THE GOLDEN BRACELET

A Memoir of Growing up in 1930s Syria

ADVANCE PRAISE FOR *THE GOLDEN BRACELET*

"A searing mother-daughter saga, totally true, totally harrowing, totally beautiful, from an era and a place that most of us know nothing about. Anahid Hagopian brings to vivid life the brutal but precious universe of her youth in pre-war Aleppo and her eventual escape to a world of freedom and fulfilment---all of this brought to publication by Anahid's own daughter, completing the cycle by delivering this narrative and its wisdom to you and me. *The Golden Bracelet* opened my eyes to way of seeing and thinking that I've never encountered anywhere else. Five stars!"

—Steven Pressfield, bestselling author of *Gates of Fire* and *The Arcadian*

"Undeniably interesting!"

—Pierre Berton, Governor General Award winner and bestselling author of *Klondike* and *The Last Spike*

"Reading my 7th grade French teacher's memoir led to many "Aha" moments for me. Unlike many teachers who taught "by the book," Mrs. Swann's teaching style was always different. My fondest memories include days where all of us students would gather around her desk and share our best jokes for her to share with her own children. She would also tell us stories about distant places and how to write our names in Arabic. Having known Mrs. Swann and reading her memoir reminds me of those wonderful times and helps me better understand her. Looking back, I realize now that she was sharing that little piece of Syria with us and that she was teaching the best kind of learning - learning through living - just as her mother had taught her. For those who didn't know her, this book is like a beautifully spoken song about a time that is long gone, in a faraway place."

—Angie Wilkinson, Former Student in Ann Swann's (Anahid Hagopian's) 7th Grade French class at Regency Acres Public School, Aurora, Ontario, Canada

Editors: Antonia Swann, Christine Gordon Manley, Evelyn Elgie

Cover design: Julie Van Huizen

Typesetting: Pei Yuan Li

Library and Archives Canada Cataloguing in Publication

Title: The golden bracelet : a memoir of growing up in 1930s Syria / by Anahid Hagopian.

Names: Hagopian, Anahid, author. Swann, Ann, author.

Identifiers: Canadiana (print) 20260238503 | Canadiana (ebook) 2026023852X | ISBN 9781834210353 (softcover) | ISBN 9781834210384 (EPUB) | ISBN 9781834210582 (PDF)

Subjects: LCSH: Hagopian, Anahid—Childhood and youth. | LCSH: Syria—History—French occupation, 1918-1946. | LCSH: Syria—Social conditions—20th century. | LCSH: Women—Syria—Social conditions—20th century. | LCSH: Women—Syria—Social life and customs—20th century. | LCSH: Syrians—Biography. | LCGFT: Autobiographies.

Classification: LCC DS98.13.H34 A3 2026 | DDC 956.9104/1092—dc23

INANNA
PUBLICATIONS & EDUCATION INC.
TORONTO, ONTARIO, CANADA
www.inanna.ca

Printed and bound in Canada

The publisher gratefully acknowledges the support of the Canada Council, Ontario Arts Council, and the Government of Canada, and Ontario Creates.

Canada Council for the Arts | Conseil des arts du Canada

ONTARIO ARTS COUNCIL
CONSEIL DES ARTS DE L'ONTARIO
an Ontario government agency
un organisme du gouvernement de l'Ontario

Canada

ONTARIO CREATES

THE GOLDEN BRACELET

A Memoir of Growing up in 1930s Syria

by Anahid Hagopian
Otherwise known as Ann Swann

Editor's Note

All events in this account are described as accurately as possible, as remembered by Anahid Hagopian. Many of the names and identifying details have been changed out of respect for those described.

Content Warning

Please note that this memoir contains descriptions of violence against children, child abuse, death, abortion, graphic violence, misogyny, and sexual assault.

For Tony

Table of Contents

Foreword

by Antonia Swann, Anahid's Daughter

What you are holding are my mother Anahid's earliest memories of growing up in Aleppo, Syria. The story is set against the distant backdrop of the Armenian Genocide and against the earliest rumblings of World War II. The Syria under which my mother grew up, during the 1930s, was initially under French mandate. By the end of the book, in the early-mid-1940s, my mother has become a young woman, the British have occupied Aleppo, and Syrian independence has been declared. During this period, women were not allowed to vote and "Western" feminist values, even for such things as wearing shorts in public, were scorned.

While this is an actual rags to riches story, it is not one found in fairy tales, as my mother's childhood was spent amidst male dominance, civil unrest, conflict, and uncertainty – including never really knowing her exact age or birthplace. Because of poverty, when my mother was very young, she was given up by her fiercely independent, single mother to be raised by nuns in an orphanage—a place that rewarded the well-off and abused those on the lower socio-economic rung of the ladder. Her mother did eventually return to collect her, and my mother writes about how the two learned to be with each other again. This is a story of the bond between mother and daughter, and of the sacrifices a mother will make to ensure her daughter's freedom and independence.

My grandmother's only wish in life was to make sure that my mother obtained what she called her "Golden Bracelet of Independence", meaning gaining freedom through education. In Aleppo, during the 1930s and 1940s, freedom through education—and most of life—was particularly difficult for girls and women. For instance, when my mother was born, she was given three birth certificates because recording her birth was inconsequential. Moreover, when my grandmother brought my very young, sickly mother to see a doctor, he recommended she be put to death as a young child mainly because she was female. Women were simply not as valuable. Knowing this, my fiercely independent grandmother wanted nothing more in life for her only daughter than the gift of education. Education was a ticket to freedom and my grandmother did everything she could to protect her daughter and seize any chances that would allow Anahid an education. This is the story of how my mother got her "Golden Bracelet".

Anahid began writing her memoir, I believe, when she was in her 30s. Then, over decades, she updated it. The one thing she always wanted in life (besides making sure that my brother and I were well looked after) was to have her story published. On Anahid's deathbed, I promised her that I would share her story with the world… and having it published has become one of my life's dreams as well. I am over the moon about it and I know my mother would be too! E!

Many of Ann Swann's former Canadian students and, of course, many general readers may well be surprised and even shocked by the descriptions in the coming pages as they, at times, reveal the harsh realities of an oppressive society especially when it comes to women. That being said, it is my sincerest hope that this book will shine light on the importance of women's rights, including what it means to society to be a "respectable" woman. I also hope it encourages us to celebrate the unique, and sometimes extraordinarily strong, bond between mothers and daughters.

Antonia Swann
Toronto, Ontario, Canada
July 17, 2026

Chapter 1

Struggling To Breathe

One of my earliest childhood memories takes me back to a hot summer evening in Aleppo, Syria, in the early 1930s, in a dingy room where my mother and I slept together. It must have been the rhythmic movement of the bed and the squeak of the bedsprings that first woke me up. I felt as though someone was attempting to suffocate me. The harder I struggled to push my head out from under the bedcovers, the harder a hand pressed it down. I gasped for air, thrashing my arms about and fighting with what little strength I possessed. Then the heaving stopped.

In the dim candlelight, I saw a man buttoning up his shirt. He then threw my mother what looked like a large silver coin, which caught the candlelight for a second. I felt hot and sticky, and I could smell candle wax and sweat and urine. The stranger's form created weird shadows behind him. I heard him say goodbye, and then he was gone. I had no idea who the man was, or how he happened to be in bed with me and with my mother.

As soon as the stranger left, my mother asked me to go and buy some pasterma, some pita bread, and some peaches. She gave me the majeed, a silver coin worth a few cents, that the man had tossed her.

I ran all the way to the Bab-El-Faraj marketplace as fast as my legs could carry me, feeling the cool evening breeze against my damp hair and dress. I ran over cobblestone paths and through a maze of narrow streets to finally arrive at the well-lit marketplace that came to life at dusk, buzzing with activity.

The merchant sat on a raffia chair, smoking a narghile. He wore a red fez, with a black tassel at the side, his huge bulk terminating in fat, slippered feet. Around me, women of all shapes and sizes strolled by, casually chatting, looking, bargaining, and some carrying infants. A little farther away, men sat cross-legged behind their counters, as they must have done since the Middle Ages, surrounded by huge sacks filled with all kinds of grains, nuts, and spices. Others huddled together in white turbans and robes, sitting on their haunches with their amber prayer beads, stroking their beards and, now and then, spitting on the ground. At the back of the store, two children played five stones under the watchful eye of an obese young woman covered in black from head to hennaed toe.

I asked the man for some pasterma, bread, and peaches, watching his lean face with fascination as he put one loaf aside. It was still warm, for he had just lifted it up from an open hearth. He then sliced some of the spiced beef and tossed it on the scales, balanced with gold-colored weights marking half a kilo, a kilo, and so on. He threw the slices into a square of flat brown paper, tossing a slice or two into his mouth while I watched hungrily. Having satisfied himself as to the exact weight, he began to fold the paper into a fascinating semi-circle of quick folds and handed it to me, along with the bread and two peaches.

The merchant eyed the majeed I handed him from the countertop, picked it up, and bit into it. He then threw me a suspicious glance as he held the coin up against the yellowish bulb over his head. After a moment of silence, his whole expression suddenly altered from impassivity to active outrage.

"Here!" he yelled, "you little bitch!" tossing the coin at me, while trying to snatch back the bags of food from my hand. "I could have you arrested for trying to pass me counterfeit money!" He slapped my face so hard that I went flying over the cobblestones. I lay there for a moment, writhing in pain, feeling as if a hand had gripped my stomach and given it a sharp twist.

As I went flying over the medieval cobblestones, so, too, did the food. The merchant reached for my hair, but I dodged him, the shock at what had happened wearing off as I quickly reacted on instinct. I lunged for the food, grabbing it, and started to run. He yelled and jumped over the countertop, reaching for my dress. I could feel his hand on the back of my neck, but I kept running. I could hear his heaving breathing as I ran, but I did not dare look behind me. I weaved in and out of the stalls, narrowly escaping his grabbing hands but still hearing his heavy breathing. Eventually, I heard him less and less. Finally, I stopped and turned around. He was gone.

Food tightly in hand, I bounded up the staircase that led up to our tiny apartment. My mother opened the door and, after I told her the story, she hugged me, then she cursed both man and creation, lamenting all the injustices women had to endure till the final flickers of the candlelight. We sat on the edge of the mattress, devouring the meat, pita bread, and peaches like two ravenous sisters; my mother was only about fifteen years older than I, and we had not eaten in three days.

Later that night, to escape paying rent, my mother and I climbed down a minuscule ladder, through the back window of our small room. We took our cat, Jimmy, with us, who cautiously descended while my mother and I waited in the eerie moonlight with our belongings bundled up at the foot of the ladder.

Chapter 2

Put Her To Sleep

Years later, when I was older, my mother explained that she had gone to bed with the stranger, albeit at the wrong time of the month, in order to get money to buy us some food, only to be paid with a counterfeit coin. She also told me she had tried to commit suicide that night by soaking match heads in water and drinking the liquid, but I had gone and put my arms around her, which she said had saved her life.

I sometimes wonder what that shopkeeper would think if he could see me today, living a middle-class life in a small town, thousands of miles away? Although I am old enough to qualify for the old age pension, having retired from my profession as a school teacher, to this day, I do not know my exact age, my real name, or where I was born. There is still a mystery surrounding my early childhood.

The times themselves were turbulent, and quickly separated the survivors from the victims. From the Armenian Massacre to the cauldron of the Second World War, the Middle East I knew was in constant turmoil.

As I look back on my topsy-turvy life, I have come to realize how much I depended on my mother—for all her faults and despite the extravagance of her opinions and her lifestyle—as a guide and even a refuge.

In the beginning, my mother and I lived in a district of Aleppo called Bustan Kulab, which in Arabic means the Garden of Dogs. It was the red-light district; we lived not too far from a brothel. We moved from apartment to apartment, fleeing harsh landlords. Invariably, as my mother told me later, they tried to seduce her, as had the owner of Hotel Baron, the largest hotel in the city where she went to seek employment.

People threw their garbage into the street, and every evening, stray cats and dogs and children would come and rummage there. Often, I would sit on the dirty steps in my smelly dress, watching animals and street urchins fight over scraps of food. I also recall the local prostitutes, heavily rouged and powdered and smelling of lovely eau de cologne, as they passed by. They always said hello in a cheerful manner. I thought they were pretty. Much later, I learned that these cheerful creatures were allowed out of the brothels only on Thursday afternoons to go see a movie. On that day, no self-respecting Syrian citizen would venture to the cinema.

I vaguely remember going to school somewhere for a few days. I remember walking a long way, through dirty narrow streets, to get to a classroom—this memory is suspended somewhere in the backwoods of my life. I don't know what the school was called or why I did not continue to attend. I could not have been more than five or six years old at the time. Education cost the earth in those days; you had to be wealthy to attend school.

Perhaps I dropped out because my mother could not afford to pay for my schooling, or it could also be that I was an anemic, sickly child. I wet my bed every night, and every day my mother hung the mattress over the balcony rails to dry in the sun. I also had lice and worms. I recall sitting on the chamber-pot pulling the long yellow, almost translucent wiggly worms out with my bare hands.

When I caught the measles and was burning with fever, my mother went to fetch a doctor, as there were no telephones in houses in those days. I could smell the fragrance of his eau de cologne before I saw him. He drew his thick black brows together while he examined me in the silent room. He told my mother I not only had measles, but also tuberculosis of the bones, that it was hopeless, and that I should be put to sleep.

The doctor even offered to take me to the general hospital in the city and give me the injection himself, but my mother refused to accept his gloomy prognosis. She explained that she could never accept euthanasia, that she would rather keep me and watch me die in her arms than send me away with him. She appreciated his visit, but she did not have enough money to pay him.

He persisted in his attempt to persuade my mother. After all, female infants were often discarded by being thrown into fireplaces or some such place. A girl was considered a curse at birth and the government usually did not bother to register their birth because they did not count as useful citizens. The doctor told my mother that she was young, vibrant, and beautiful—she would fare better without having me as a burden.

Seeing her poverty, the doctor wondered whether he could pay her a personal visit from time to time, as he found her very attractive. Instead of sending her a bill, he went to bed with her. Years later, when things got better, my mother described her deep repugnance of that physician, and that she paid more in humiliation and tears than any monies owed.

Unknown to me at the time, it was at that moment in my childhood when my mother realized she could not take care of me by herself, and that was why she handed me over to the care of the nuns at the Franciscan orphanage. There, at least, the nuns would feed me once a day, while she tried to survive on her own as best she could.

Chapter 3

Number 86

An imposing building, the Franciscan Orphanage was financed by a wealthy widow. It stood miles outside the city, on top of a hill. At the time when I was sent there, Syria was still under French mandate.

Suddenly, I found myself deprived of my mother's warm and loving presence, thrust into this immense, cold institution with women in uniforms. Only their faces, necks, and hands exposed, reminding me of the local ladies I used to see at the marketplace. The expressions in the nuns' eyes were cool and distant, and their voices were quiet and controlled, almost emotionless. For a long time, I could not remember how I came to be at the orphanage. I felt abandoned, but in my heart I knew that my mother never intended to abandon me. To realize that was, for a long time, my only consolation.

The center of the building consisted of the main chapel, the wine cellar, and a chic drawing room with red velvet curtains that hosted visiting dignitaries who came from as far away as Rome, Paris, and Buenos Aires. The convent itself was divided into two wings, housing radically different groups of children: those of the wealthy, who were chauffeur-driven to school every day, and the orphans or the destitute, who performed all the necessary chores, catering to the rich children's needs.

The orphans were the janitorial staff, and I was one of them. We weren't allowed to mingle with the rich girls. We cleaned their classrooms, as well as the hallways; under the vigilant eyes of the nuns, about twice a year, we worked at the main entrance, making sure that everything was kept clean and impressive and that the front gardens were well-manicured.

We were given two sets of underwear, a pair of black shoes, a gray uniform, and a pair of black socks, all duly numbered. We were also each given a number. Mine was 86. Our last names were not used because most of us did not know them.

I befriended Number 72, whose name was Josephine, because she was about my age. We were divided into two groups, and she and I belonged to the same group. I also liked Louise, number 45, a fine girl with reddish blonde curls and a pretty face, who was in charge of the younger group and who performed the more delicate chores, such as ironing and folding uniforms.

The lower corridors, where we walked and performed some of our manual work, were gray cement, and so was our refectory. The dormitories were situated on two separate floors and contained single metal beds. The four corners of both dormitories were occupied by supervising nuns. Each corner was draped off into a cubicle, much like those seen in hospitals. We later discovered that the nuns had tiny little slits in the curtains in order to keep an eye on us while we slept.

It was like living in a black and white silent movie, for we rarely spoke or socialized in the normal sense of the word. We weren't allowed to sit in small groups and talk, but, then, there was little time for idle chatter. We weren't there to play as other children do—we were there to work and to justify our presence. After all, we were being fed gratis. Besides, the nuns did not believe in wasting time on things like fun and games.

It was a world of silence, obedience, and work. It was always, "Oui, ma mère," or, "Oui, ma soeur." The word *non* did not exist, as far as we were concerned. Not only did we learn to speak Parisian French, but we also learned to speak it in whispers.

The nuns were supposed to be some sort of surrogate sisters or mothers, but during all my years at the orphanage, I have no recollection of seeing a nun laugh or hug an orphan, and I never saw a nun cry. It seemed their habits not only covered their bodies all the way down to their toes, but they also served to hide their emotions. We were never permitted to throw our arms around their necks and hug them. If I happened to be mopping up the marble corridors on the rich girls' side and the Mother Superior walked by, I was expected to step back, bow reverentially, and whisper, "Bonjour, ma mère."

I can still feel the slight breeze and the jingling of the heavy iron cross. I would never dare look the Mother Superior in the eye, too afraid to stir the solemn slumber of the vast, cold sanctuary. Statues of St. Joseph, St. Paul, St. Theresa, or of the Virgin Mary, as well as dozens of others, stood almost as mutely and as frigidly as some of the nuns themselves. In a sense, they all seemed like monuments dedicated to the next world.

We enacted the Stations of the Cross, going from one scene to another, on our knees, like frantic amputees, each one of us bearing her own respective cross—for the orphanage, with its glittering marble floors, had become our Via Dolorosa, our Painful Path. I remember witnessing the marriage of a nun to Jesus; we watched the novice wear the wedding ring and don the crown of thorns. The solemnity of these ceremonies held little or no significance for me; I think I was too young to appreciate the subtleties of religious indoctrination. However, if any of the orphans revealed a penchant for a dedication to a life of divine service, then that orphan was considered for the novitiate and, subsequently, given the higher academic learning worthy of a Roman Catholic.

A handful of us were admitted into the church choir, where we sang Latin hymns, such as "Ave Marie Stella," "Veni Creator Spiritus," and "Ave Maria," as well as some French hymns like, "Jésus, Marie, Joseph, je vous donne mon coeur," "C'est le mois de Marie," or "Je suis Chrétien, voilà ma gloire." It all sounded beautiful, much like Elizabethan madrigals, especially the Latin hymns, which I loved and enjoyed. A counterpoint to these enchanting hymns was the clatter in our refectory, of tin mugs and plates and our muffled footsteps as we went about our daily chores.

Despite frequent movement and activity during the waking hours, if I were to shut my eyes, I could easily imagine the long corridors, the dormitories, and even the refectories to be almost empty, it was that quiet. The nuns were our constant and vigilant supervisors and guides. We followed their orders all day long, every minute of the day, until we were led to our dormitories. The lifestyle zapped all the emotion from me, either from fatigue or disillusionment or perhaps a blend of both. I recall lying in bed, after a hard day of scrubbing floors or other chores, wondering where my mother was. There were no tears in my eyes. I merely wondered where she was. I felt I was not so much registered at the orphanage, as sentenced, for it was to become the fortress that cramped my natural self and left an insidious imprint on my soul.

Chapter 4

'Unhappinesses' In My Heart

We were roused at six o'clock every morning to wash in cold water (both in winter and in summer). After kneeling by our beds to say a short prayer, we were then walked down to the chapel to hear mass, conducted by a priest. That was when we sang with the nuns in the morning choir. After that, we were given our respective chores to perform.

One of my jobs was to sort sacks full of lentils or rice, sitting on a chair placed under an electric light, in one of the hallways leading to the refectory—a task that took a few days to accomplish. Another regular chore I was assigned was the washing of five hundred nuns' handkerchiefs every Thursday afternoon. I would soak them in cold water for a while, brush off the mucus into a bucket placed beside me, throw the sopping mess into a cauldron of boiling water, and then wash each handkerchief by hand...one by one.

Also, we carried buckets of coal to the cellar, and, on rare occasions, we watched the nuns with the older orphans make candles in the basement. We would dye pebbles and help to decorate the main entrance for all the rich girls' parents to admire. I remember it was the only colorful chore at the orphanage. Everything else was as drab and as dull as the lives we led.

All day, every minute of the day, we were told to do certain things. We were ordered, guided, or led. I had no sense of the passage of time, so I began to invent my own inner clock—in color. Mornings were pale yellow, noon hours were orange red, and evenings, the saddest of all, I designated as black. My minutes, hours, and days were all color-coded. Neither the clock nor the conventional calendar meant anything to me. I went by colors during the day, and by the moon at night, for I could not escape its presence in the sky from where I lay in my dormitory bed. I believed that I religiously followed the phases of the moon.

I frequently, yet quietly cried myself to sleep under the bedcovers, calling for my mother. I never stopped wondering where she was, and I had no idea of how long it had been since I had last seen her lovely face. What made it harder for me was the fact that other orphans received the odd visitor on Sunday afternoons.

One Sunday night, while crying myself to sleep, a couple of lines of verse came into my head, out of nowhere. The lines were in French, since French was the language we orphans, and everyone else, spoke. What Armenian or Turkish words or sentences were left in my memory seemed to have evaporated by then. French had become my mother tongue. I knew nothing about poetry or rhyme—education was not the primary goal for the orphans. Yes, the nuns did teach us how to read and write, told us Biblical stories, and showed us illustrated copies of events while we were in our classrooms, but those periods were not too frequent. I can't say how often we attended classes, but I know that they did not seem to be regularly available.

It seems odd that the few lines I composed while lying in bed, thinking of my mother, still remain with me. In spite of its poor grammar, it said something about my feelings. The English version of those humble lines could be translated as follows:

"It is six o'clock/I have unhappinesses in my heart."

The original version in French says:

"Il est six heures/J'ai des malheurs dans mon coeur."

Even though it rhymes in French, the word "unhappinesses," which is "malheurs" in French, is just as incorrect in French as it is in English.

Chapter 5

Je recule pour mieux sauter

One hot, dull afternoon, I saw two nuns run to open the huge, heavy, wooden doors, giving unto the vast, arid recreation grounds at the back of the convent, on our side of the orphanage. It was, we were told, the fourth Sunday of the month—a visiting day. It took the nuns quite a bit of physical effort and time to get those great big doors open. It was the door that we orphans had walked through once or twice to see a part of the outside world, as we were marched quietly, in single file, over dry and deserted areas.

On that memorable Sunday, as I sat alone on a stone, watching lizards dart from under rocks, I thought I saw someone walk slowly towards me, someone who vaguely resembled my mother. She was carrying a small suitcase.

I kept looking in her direction, blinking in the sun. As the figure loomed larger, I saw that she was smiling at me. How beautiful she looked, and how smartly dressed she was. I was afraid to move, to get up, in case I was imagining the whole scene, for I had often secretly thought how wonderful it would be if only my Maman would walk through those huge doors and take me home with her. But that dream, or whatever it was, had worn thin with time.

"Maman?" I mumbled.

"Yes, my darling," she responded, and took me in her arms while a flood of tears streamed down her cheeks wetting my face. "Oh, my love! How I missed you!"

Before I could speak again, she blew her nose, wiped her eyes, and, as if reading my mind, she added, still holding me tightly, "I got a ride today, I came with Madame Flora. I will not be able to take you home, not yet, my love, but I hope to do so sometime in the future."

"Oh, Maman, Maman," I cried, "can't I go home with you now?"

"No, my sweetheart," she replied, wiping her beautiful hazel eyes. She added a sentence I have never forgotten to this day: "Je recule pour mieux sauter, ma chérie." *I am taking a step back in order to better leap forward, my darling.*

She distributed some treats among a handful of orphans, keeping a large supply for me. She kept wiping her eyes, nose, and cheeks and tried to cheer me up by telling me that things were getting better, that she would return to visit me as soon as she could, and that I should be patient… that the day would come when she would take me home for good.

My mother's visit made it harder for me to bear her absence. The food that she had brought was gone that same day; I shared it with the rest of my friends. I use the term *friends* loosely, for we barely spoke to one another, except to exchange a few words relating to our respective chores, yet I have one memory of two orphans skipping rope quietly and seemingly having fun. Other than that scene, there was hardly any laughter or shouting as is normal when children play.

With time, I fell back into the daily routine of working, eating, praying, and sleeping. For a long time, the visitors' doors continued to open and close without my mother walking through them. I would sit close to the entrance, staring at the huge, wooden doors, hoping that, any minute now, she would appear before me.

Once those doors were shut, they shut out any hope I had of seeing my mother again. And it would be a long time before they would re-open, and who knows if she would walk through them again. I went to bed night after night feeling I had no one in the world to love me.

Chapter 6

Biting Into Cockroaches

In a country where the average person was, at the time, barely on subsistence level, we orphans were among the "fortunate." We were fed regularly enough, but the emphasis was always on the state of our souls. We were fed more Pater Nosters, more Ave Marias, than beans. Those of us who worked hard and behaved well were rewarded with leftover food. We drank water and black tea from tin mugs.

Biting into cockroaches and spitting them out was not an uncommon occurrence. I remember biting and spitting them out as casually as if they were prune pits, a regimen that greatly assisted me in my future life, for I developed a strong constitution and a strong stomach.

Part of our daily rigid discipline included the way we sat at the refectory table. Our posture was important. I well recall a senior nun pricking me in the back with her long cornet-pin to remind me to sit up straight. To this day, I feel uneasy about people standing behind me (and my posture still leaves much to be desired).

One memorable day, we were served black-eyed beans for lunch. They smelled awful. Around my neck hung a pair of long socks belonging to one of the nuns—I hadn't finished darning the second one, so she had hung it around my neck for me to finish the work during afternoon recess. I tried to eat the food before me, but it made me feel sick. The supervising nun soon noticed that I was not eating my lunch. She was behind me like a shot. She wanted to know why I was not eating. I explained that I felt sick. She insisted I try. She took the tablespoon, filled it with the rotten beans and made me open my mouth so she could shove the whole thing in. I forced myself to chew and swallow, but my gorge was rising. I was afraid of the nun, and I was even more afraid of being sick all over the table. She got another spoonful and again ordered me to open my mouth.

"Mademoiselle, mademoiselle, you can, if you try!" she said. That was when I vomited all over my plate, feeling a terrible pain in the pit of my stomach. It felt as if the refectory was twisting around like a Ferris wheel.

The nun was disgusted with my behavior. She insisted I eat my lunch and that she would accept no excuses and that I would serve as an example to the rest of the orphans who were now taking an interest in what was happening. She gave me my plate of beans, vomit and all, with the tablespoon to take outside. I was to march along with the rest of the girls on to the recreation grounds carrying my unfinished lunch.

I can still see myself walking. The other girls were afraid of getting involved. Close bonds of any kind were discouraged anyway; there was not a soul to whom I could have turned.

The sun beat down on me, hitting the top of my head like an iron poker. I remember my head felt as if it was going to crack into pieces. Strange how some memories still linger, while others, perhaps far more significant, fade into oblivion. But that day was one I can never forget. I know one thing for sure—none of the nuns came to see what was wrong when I collapsed. No one inquired whether I was sick or dying.

I was glad, in a way, to be left alone, to be left lying there, on the recreation grounds. I must have subconsciously felt that I did not care whether I lived or died. When a bell rang in the distance, my whole being responded because, after all, we were guided by bells. I was lying in a pool of sweat and vomit under that terrible heat. I remember hearing that bell, when everything went black.

Chapter 7

Kind Blue Eyes

When I opened my eyes, I found myself in the infirmary with a sister taking my temperature. She seemed to be smiling at me, or was I imagining it? At least her blue eyes looked kindly at me. She held the thermometer to the window light and explained that I had a bit of a temperature and that I had passed out during afternoon recess. Then she told me to shut my eyes and rest.

I cannot say how many days I spent at the infirmary, but I know that a few days later I had chewed some gum in bed, given to me by number 72, via Madame Flora (her mother). The gum had stuck to my right temple, and I had a job trying to pull it out of my hair. I was terrified lest the nun punish me for it. I was crying and tugging at my hair when the nun held my hand, squeezed it reassuringly, smiling down at me. She then brought out a pair of scissors and cut off the whole area, explaining that I could have choked on the gum, that I should not chew gum in bed for my own safety. There was not the slightest hint of anger in her voice.

I had never seen that nun before. I wondered why she was never on our side of the convent. She was so gentle and kind; she reminded me a little of my mother. Although I never got to know her name, I have never forgotten her kind and gentle manner.

As soon as I was well enough to leave the infirmary, there was a punishment awaiting me. I was to serve as an example to the rest of the orphans. I was given a placard to wear that read: "Je suis une fille désobéissante" (I am a disobedient girl), and I was to walk the recreation grounds wearing it both during morning and afternoon recess.

How I wished I were ill so that I could see that lovely nun again! My time at the infirmary had been the happiest of my life at the orphanage. Unfortunately, I was not destined to see her again. Instead, I was ordered to carry that placard under the indifferent eye of the supervising nun and the scorching summer sun, over the rough, barren recreation grounds.

Years and years later, when I happened to see workers on strike, I never failed to remember that distant scene at the orphanage with me carrying the sign that proclaimed to the orphanage at large that I was, indeed, a disobedient girl. It was my punishment for not eating the rotten, black-eyed beans.

Chapter 8

The Cellar

One morning, during mass, as Josephine and I knelt side-by-side, instead of praying, we were discussing a plan of escape. We decided to stash our soiled clothing items for a week since we had only two sets, and then make a dash for the great big wooden doors, climb over them, and escape to freedom. It did not occur to us what we would do afterwards, or how we would find our respective mothers. We were young and naïve; in our minds, the plan seemed certain to succeed.

On the night of our escape, we waited until we were supposed to be in our beds, asleep, and then snuck out, barefoot, making a dash for the dormitory door. We got as far as the main floor exit when two nuns shouted for us to stop, and that was the end of our attempt at running away. They took our bundles from us and marched us back to our respective beds, which were in different corners of the same floor, with the threat of severe punishment.

We had already washed blocked toilet bowls with our bare hands, we had scrubbed dirty floors with cold water, we were used to humiliation tactics, and we had been deprived of recreation time. Now, we wondered what punishment could possibly be waiting in store for us next.

The next day, we were both dismissed from our chores—something that had never happened to any other orphan that we knew of—and were marched down to a small room in the basement by two nuns carrying a set of keys. They let us both in and locked the door behind us without saying a single word. As we discovered that evening, the basement harbored mice, rats, and cockroaches; the place smelled awful.

The floor consisted of rough soil, similar to our recreation grounds. A narrow window, close to the ceiling, let in some light. Neither of us could utter a word, we were that petrified. We also didn't cry.

We sat huddled together wondering what was going to happen. We waited and we waited. We lost track of time. The sky began to darken. No one came to turn on the lights. No one came to give us any food or water. We felt small. Darting objects around us made faint squeaking noises; we dared not make the slightest move.

We remained huddled together until the first flickers of dawn. I don't know if we slept at all, I can't remember. Once enough light entered so that we could see, we noticed that the electric bulb above our heads had been removed. We wouldn't have been able to turn on the lights, even if we had been able to find the light switch in the dark.

The first day came and went. The sky darkened once again. We were terrified that no one would ever return to see what happened to us. We lost the ability to talk. We stopped thinking about food or using the bathroom—we simply waited for the door to open. We strained our ears to listen for footsteps, and, every so often, we would eye the small window close to the ceiling. But no one came.

The following afternoon, two young nuns walked in, laughing and joking. I had never heard a nun laugh before—the only one I could ever imagine laughing was the gentle nun who cared for me when I was ill. These young nuns were holding a mouse they had caught and put in a cage. One kept poking it with a hatpin sending it squeaking to the other side of the cage, while the other nun sent it back again. Each took turns pricking the mouse and laughing each time it came towards her. It was like a ping-pong game for them.

Josephine and I stood in a corner feeling sick. The nuns acted as though we were not even there. No food or water was given to us. When we were eventually allowed to leave, early that evening, I felt weak and dizzy.

My experience in the cellar made me think of number 45, Louise, and wondering if she, too, might also have spent some time there. I remember Louise always carried a handkerchief with her and blew her nose frequently during mass in the chapel. Was she crying? I did not know. At night, when we were all in bed, she would shout uncontrollably, while the whole wing of the orphanage listened in mute terror. She kept saying, in French, of course, "Ah! Les mouches! Les mouches!" ("Ah! The flies! The flies!") And then she would scream, "Aidez-moi! Aidez-moi!" ("Help me! Help me!") and, "J'ai peur!" ("I'm afraid!") Her cries haunted me for a long time. We could all hear Louise's terrified screams rising all the way to our dormitories, sending chills through us. But no one dared mutter a sound.

We never did discover the reason for Louise's screams. One night they just stopped. No one ever saw her again or knew where she went. I never did find out what became of her or what must have terrified her so.

Chapter 9

Beautiful Stranger

As time passed and things went on dully as usual, I began to dream less and less of my mother. I felt that she would never return, that I would end up working as a maid somewhere. Yet, at times, I could not help wondering what could have happened to her.

One afternoon, during recess, those orphans who had worked hard and obeyed all the rules were given a picture of Saint Theresa by one of the senior nuns. It was a black and white headshot. I sat and watched the nun from a short distance, while Josephine stood by quietly. Each orphan was told to stare at the picture and, without blinking, count up to one hundred and immediately look up at the sky to see the mystic's face in the heavens. This was the ultimate reward for good behavior. Naturally, I was deprived of the pleasure of this religious experience because I was a bad girl, and so was Josephine. We watched an older orphan marvel at the so-called miracle.

Perhaps I had been yearning for the wrong kind of miracle, for as I aimlessly wandered about the grounds, wishing that I could see what the other girl was marveling at, I caught sight of a woman dressed in black. She did not come through the huge wooden doors reserved for the poor parents of orphans, but rather via the tennis courts where the rich, day students, dressed in white shorts, played tennis with the nuns. We were not allowed to watch them.

The blinding white habits of the nuns and the white shorts and tops of the carefree, giggling girls contrasted with the black costume of the beautiful stranger who was walking towards me. I did not see the back of the car until the Mother Superior beckoned me with her index finger from a distance. I wondered what I had done wrong this time as I walked sheepishly towards the tall, elderly nun in white standing beside the smartly dressed young lady in black.

I was trembling. The Mother Superior spoke to me, not unkindly, I thought. She told me to kneel down and apologize for my sins of disobedience. Her voice quivered with authority. I looked at her pale, implacable face and faded gray eyes for the first time. She repeated her order.

I found myself kneeling at her feet on the rough ground, just like a camel under its rider's weight and whip, and mouthed the words of contrition, as I was accustomed to doing in the chapel.

The holy mother then lifted the long beads catching the black iron crucifix and brought it to my lips to kiss. She then blessed me and forgave me and told me to get up, that she had news for me.

The visitor in black watched all this in silence. Every few seconds, she sniffled. I rubbed the dust off my knees and stood up. I was not sure who the person was. It could not have been my mother, and, yet, her eyes seemed to be the eyes I remembered. I wondered why she was so quiet. She kept looking at me while dabbing her cheeks with a handkerchief.

The Mother Superior spoke again, looking at me, "Your mother has come to take you out." And, turning to the lady in black, she added, "Please follow me, Madame."

The stranger in black then embraced me, a cool and welcoming perfume emanating from her. She couldn't speak. She kept wiping her nose with a lace handkerchief with some initials on it. She was so beautiful—how happy I was to be her daughter!

I was fascinated by the Napoleon hat, which I later discovered had been especially designed for her, as well as the black costume, and the black, hand-made shoes. And the beautiful red rose. Oh how lovely and how red that red rose was! Was I really leaving the orphanage? I was in a state of utter disbelief.

I left the Franciscan orphanage that day. On the following Monday, I was registered on the rich girls' side, privileged to tread the very marble floors I scrubbed for so many years. The details of my registration escape me, but I will never forget the ride home that fateful afternoon—the chauffeur-driven car and my mother sitting beside me, still holding her handkerchief to her face, and every so often, wiping her beautiful eyes. I just sat there staring ahead most of the time and watching the arid scenery roll by, as if in a strange dream. I remember counting telegraph poles as the car made its way towards some new and extraordinary destination.

Chapter 10

A World Of Luxury

After being plucked from the prison of an orphanage so lacking in love it would make Dickens's harsh and desolate Dotheboys Hall of Nicholas Nickleby seem like a fairyland, I was suddenly transported into what, by comparison, appeared to be the most luxurious surroundings.

I could not believe my eyes when the car finally stopped outside the house. Inside, I beheld my bedroom in wonder, with its double bed, quilted pink satin covers, a desk and chairs, a bookshelf, and a small green plant in one corner. It also had a small balcony overlooking a clean and wide street.

My mother's bedroom was larger. She had a canopied bed with mosquito netting that flowed down on each side like a work of art. The bedcover, which appeared to be made out of leopard skin, was soft to the touch. The linen sheets were all hand-embroidered, as I learned later on, and each had her initials on them. It was the same with the matching pillowcases.

The walls were mostly covered with small Persian rugs. There were some odd-looking pictures on the walls depicting a woman in fancy clothes. I soon learned that this was my mother as an actress. Also, in her bedroom, great big velour cushions were thrown here and there casually, depicting scenes from French history.

One, for example, showed Napoléon Bonaparte with Joséphine in an amorous pose against a sweeping background of beautiful gardens worthy of a Gainsborough painting. Hand-painted flowers of the most delicate violet and fern-green hues graced her curtains. Whenever the wooden shutters were thrown open at sunset, those curtains waved in the breeze like so many hanging plants. I could almost smell them.

Her wardrobe, commode, bed, night table, and chairs, as well as her two divans and one love seat, were all of the same wood and design.

When we stood together in front of the long rectangular mirror, I saw a beautiful young woman smiling at an emaciated child of about eight years old, in shabby clothes. I stared back, wide-eyed, devouring my own reflection with fascination and awe, as I had never seen my own face in a mirror before. There were no mirrors at the orphanage—though I could sometimes see a reflection of myself in a glass doorway or in a window-pane.

So many questions circulated in my mind. What had happened to my mother all the time I was in the orphanage? How did she come to have all this money? Was this a dream? Was I really home?

Chapter 11

A Glass Of Water

The following Monday after my mother had come to get me, Maurice (our chauffeur) drove me to the school where I had been an orphan, identified only two days earlier as number 86. Now, I walked in step with the wealthiest, most powerful people's children in the elegant wing where I had never been allowed to linger longer than my chores necessitated. After school, I was driven back home.

Both our house and the school seemed like a dream. I could not quite shake the sense of unreality that enveloped me.

The colors in our house impressed me the most, for I had become so accustomed to shades of gray and black. The red roses in a Venetian glass vase, the opaque white globe of the lamps shot with the most delicate green and pale purple to the deepest reds and tinted pinks, the tall corner tables with their deep, shiny green plants, and, oh, so many others.

And the scent of my mother's perfumes or eau de cologne was amazing. Jean-Marie Farina… Lucien Lelong… Eau de Quinine… 47ll… Coty… Houbigant… The beautiful bottles stood like crystal regiments on her night table. She possessed not one of each, but sets of them in rows, according to their make and size. The sharp cinnamon scent of her Eau de Quinine never left me, for she used it daily after having her hair shampooed at home. Roses, too, never fail to take me back even after so many decades. Her Pond's face powder and her huge Parisian, pink powder-puffs were a constant source of pleasure. Her variegated, colored soaps of various shapes and sizes were also a source of sheer delight. I would hold the pale pink bars, some heart-shaped or flower-like, and inhale, with closed eyes, their lovely, elusive perfume, deeply into my soul.

The aroma of the local cuisine was another source of pleasure. Our cook, Elias, had been lured from a French colonel's services, and paid double, in order to come and cook for us. His prime concern was to be my health. I was to be fattened up, according to my mother's order. I was never to eat the same meal twice within two weeks. Consequently, Elias prepared his menu with caution, subject to my mother's approval, and he was to become one of the busiest private cooks in the city.

The first meal I remember sharing with my mother privately was when we were served a magnificently cooked leg of lamb. I reached for a slab of butter that Elias had set down on the table in a separate dish. As I was about to bite a huge chunk of it, my mother, in her normal, gentle manner, held my hand and said, "Darling, this is not cheese, this is butter. It is all fat. You only eat a tiny bit of it, spread over a slice of baguette." She then took the huge slab from my hand and put it back in the butter dish after showing me how.

Elias could perform culinary miracles. His excellent efforts were never wasted, for we often had generals and ministers' aides, judges, lawyers, and other professional men at our table. His most extraordinary dish, which would astonish any gourmet, was probably his broiled chicken. He could take out most of the bones in an entire chicken and place it on the decorated platter for the guests to cut off any of its parts without striking a single large or medium size bone. I have never seen it done since, and I have dined in many highly respectable restaurants in Europe and in the Middle East. At any rate, delicious aromas permeated our kitchen. His cakes, tortes, pies, and parfaits were all miracles of fine cuisine.

On Elias' days off, my mother would send our servant, Marie, to order the delivery of some shish kebab. The appetizing aroma of the shish kebab traveled the district like a genie on fire. The half-burnt and softened liquid tomatoes, wrapped in bread, the chopped spring onions with their variegated shades of green, with the white on one side and the green on the other; the green peppers and the burnt and wrinkled bright red peppers, were all added to the delicate dish. The parsley strewn over all this made it a real garden of delight.

One day, weeks after I had left the orphanage, my mother saw me raise my hand to ask Elias for a glass of water, saying, in French, for I knew no other language at the time, "Puis-je avoir un verre d'eau, s'il vous plait, Monsieur Elias?"

She stopped dead in her tracks, puzzled by my gesture. When I repeated the request with my accustomed humble courtesy, she asked why I had raised my hand to ask for a glass of water. I explained that that was the way we were told to behave at the orphanage. She then looked quizzically at Elias, smiled, and told me that I was no longer at the orphanage, that I no longer needed to raise my hand to ask for anything of anybody. She assured me, in front of our cook, that all I had to do was to give the order and that my wish would be satisfied, for as long as she lived.

Chapter 12

Hosanna

I had been transported from the austere world of nuns to a world of men; from a world of whispers and prayers to a world of loud and often zestful music; and from the drab world of black-and-white-and-gray to a world bursting with color.

My new existence was full of excitement and change. All this had replaced the monotony and the fear of the years spent at the orphanage, and it was in sharp contrast to the virginal hymns of the angelic voices of the Roman Catholic choir of the orphanage. Operas, farces, operettas, tragedies of all sorts were all acted and re-enacted, rehearsed, and re-rehearsed before my bewildered eyes and ears. Actors, or performers of any kind, seemed to be extroverted. I found myself amused for hours, listening to their witty repartees and frank comments, or watching their histrionic behavior. The music was beautiful and the rehearsals were fun. I loved every minute of it.

My mother was making her living as an actress and a dancer. There was still some slight stigma attached to the profession, even though the area was still under French mandate and a single woman could make her living by performing on the stage. On the whole, she was highly respected and loved by many.

Her stage presence was electric. She was also an incorrigible thespian off stage. Her idol was Rosine Bernard, otherwise known as Sarah Bernhardt. She acted in many parts the French actress had performed, such as la Dame aux camélias. She never stopped raving about Sarah Bernhardt and flattered the great actress by emulation. She also acted the part of Cordelia in Shakespeare's King Lear, and Tosca, and so many others I can't remember. She also belly-danced during some seasons and sang in Turkish, Arabic, Armenian, and Greek, as well as translations of famous works. My mother's talent as an actress was greatly admired and her ability to play several different musical instruments and sing and act stood her in good stead during all the years that followed.

She would often entertain and delight me when we were alone by singing "Viens, le soir descend," or "Plaisir d'amour." I still don't know who wrote those marvelous songs, for there were so many, and even if I did, I could not remember them all. Also, she would read me translations of all kinds of novels, detective stories, biographies, and so on.

By the standards of those days, my mother was considered a real beauty. Men seemed to prefer somewhat plump and fair-skinned women like her. And she used her looks effectively. Her self-assurance and her phenomenal memory also formed part of her success. She could memorize a whole play or an operetta within a few weeks. And the timing of her lines, along with her extraordinary patience with the various members of the cast, or orchestra, as well as her meticulous attention to the minutest detail delineated by her close friend and director, Aram, worked wonders on the stage. Together, they would go over a particular scene, again and again, until it was perfect. I would watch quietly in a corner, wide-eyed, taking in the wonderful world of actors. The intricacies, the subtleties of any one word, or movement, were remarkable.

She loved tragedies, but she also had a strong comedic vein. When she acted in sad parts, she became so deeply immersed in the given role that, for days afterwards, she would feel depleted and depressed. When she acted the part of Queen Gertrude,

Desdemona, or young Juliet, she could not sleep for days, and a period of adjustment was essential. It is probable that her choice of tragic plays was alternated with the comedies of Molière and others, for this very reason.

She was in constant demand, except during some summer months when we went away together on holidays, but her time was always well organized. When I was able to see more of her, I began to notice and learn more about her personal style of life.

My mother's wardrobe, which was huge, contained almost every imaginable outfit and design, including magnificent belly-dance costumes and sequined head-dresses and a whole array of fantastic Shakespearian or French outfits befitting the great roles she played. Her lavish costumes always fascinated me. I could write a whole book to describe her clothes alone. She wore magnificent low-cut gowns and negligés. She seemed to have a costume for every occasion, depending on the role she was playing at the time and the theatre in which she was performing.

Her dressmaker, Charlotte, was often taken, who knows how many times, to see the same particular movie, not for entertainment, but so that she could copy the marvelous modern fashions Hollywood stars were exhibiting to the world in those days. And if Charlotte did not get it right after seeing the movie once, back she would go again and again till my mother was satisfied that she had an exact copy of the outfit.

Even her pajamas were a source of amazement. One day, my mother decided to have a pair of pajamas made in the red, white, and blue of the French flag, but with the silk material only one inch wide, and cut on a bias. It must have been akin to making a hand-made quilt and caused poor Charlotte days of nightmare, for it is not easy to cut silk on a bias, into long and narrow strips and try to sew them together, one inch at a time, one by one, on her hand-operated Singer sewing-machine. But when they were finally made, the pajamas looked superb and Charlotte was generously compensated for her efforts.

Another pair of pajamas—far easier to make—consisted of an off-white silk material with pearl buttons, but again, with a difference. The buttons went all the way down the outside of her pant leg so that she could take them off simply by unbuttoning each outer side—the whole front and back pieces would come off separately, like two sheets of paper.

Because her career meant late nights—often, she wouldn't come home until the early hours of the morning— my mother slept late. She usually had breakfast in bed around noon, to coincide with my own lunch hour. Marie took a silver tray up to her, and I would kiss her good morning before Elias served me my lunch, alone, at the dining room table. I ate quickly in order to get back to the Franciscan school in time because Maurice had a long way to drive.

In spite of her extravagant lifestyle, my mother neither drank nor smoked. She was, however, addicted to Turkish coffee. It had to be black, sweet, and thick, and she consumed about twenty or thirty cups a day.

Chapter 13

The Acrobats

When I returned from school, I usually found the house empty, for she would already have left for the theatre. Elias made me my dinner, while Marie went home to see to her two daughters. I would not see my mother until the next day at noon hour, unless she was between shows or on holiday. The more successful she became, the less and less I began to see of her.

Occasionally, when I had no school, I was permitted to accompany her to the theatre, where I was protected from view by a trellised corner. There, I sat and watched her perform without being seen by the audience. At times, I was joined in my cubicle by performers my mother found to be congenial, such as the family of acrobats from northern Italy, who bore the incongruous Slavic surname of Nikovich. Both the Nikovich parents and their two daughters, Vanda and Ida, were blonde. I watched them with great fascination, for they were quite extraordinary acrobats.

It was from them that I learned how to juggle with three tennis balls and picked up the rudiments of Spanish dancing as well as the use of the castanets. Although the Nikovich girls were quite a bit older than I was, we had a great time together while they were on tour in the city. The girls became so fond of me that they asked my mother if I could join their group and travel with them, but my mother told them that she had better plans for my future than seeing me spend my life flying on the trapeze.

It was a dangerous enterprise. When Ida was five, she'd fallen from the trapeze. She had a string attached to her ankle, long enough for her father to hold from behind the curtains. It made her feel more confident, she told me. The string was not strong enough to save her from the fall, but it did apparently give her the psychological support she needed.

I would often marvel at twenty-year-old Vanda, who could bend her body into a perfect C-shape, her four limbs acting as the four legs of a table, her belly serving as the tabletop. Ida would stand on it, then leap into the air, head first, do a triple somersault, and then land on her feet beside her sister. It was while performing this same act that Ida had fallen years earlier. Her father took the string and kissed it while smiling and trying to make me laugh. Ida told me this story in her broken French. And she taught me a few Italian words because I loved the music of the language.

I much preferred their company to spending time alone at home, and my mother trusted the Nikovich family, so I was allowed to go to the theatre whenever I liked, provided I had done my homework. Inevitably, the day came when they had to move on. I never saw them again.

Chapter 14

The Players

Of course, life in the theatre was constantly changing. And new faces were emerging all the time. One member of the band was a blind violinist by the name of Barkev, who came to rehearse at our house most afternoons. I shall never forget him. Two large pins held back Barkev's abundant growth of wavy hair, just above the left eyebrow, over his dark glasses. They seemed to flow on top of his large, eyeless head, like dark sea waves drowning a pale and fragile rock.

He carried his black violin case and his white cane with him everywhere. This remarkable violinist, who gave me a handful of candies each time he came for rehearsals, would take out his pocket-watch, feel it with his fingertips, then decide whether it was time to bring out his violin and the large, white handkerchief he tucked under his chin while playing. If there was time, he would turn in the direction of my mother's voice or her fragrant perfume, and compliment her on her appearance, saying how well she must have slept the previous night, adding with a smile, "and alone." This never failed to make her chuckle.

It was hard to believe that Barkev was blind. If he needed a glass of water or some orange juice, or to use the bathroom, he would excuse himself and guide himself by lightly touching the walls, avoiding the furniture and the people around him. At times, he would sit, Sphinx-like, smiling at some inner thought, and then he would turn abruptly in my direction and say, "Little girl, why are you staring at me? Didn't the nuns teach you that it is rude to stare?"

I would look at him incredulously, wondering how on earth this totally blind musician could see so well. I would look away at once, but Barkev would always see me before I saw him. Unfortunately, Barkev, too, was destined to leave us. He got married and decided to go to Russian Armenia, where so many other Armenians were going in those days. We missed his cheerful presence.

Another unforgettable character was the clarinetist, Nersess, who was a podgy, sanguine sort of a fellow, whose closest friend was his clarinet. He would make his clarinet cry or laugh. We could all tell that Nersess and his clarinet were impatient to see my mother back on the stage again.

Aram, the director, was a perfectionist who made my mother work hard. He would stand in our large living room and lecture her on the finer points in her performance, and every step, every look, every word, every turn of the head was repeated until Aram was finally satisfied.

The death scene in Othello, for instance, almost drove my mother insane. She lay there, ready to sleep and then be murdered, only for Aram to yell, "Wrong! Wrong! Wrong! Wrong! Wrong! You don't look asleep! You look as if you're expecting to get killed." And so he pretended to be a sleeping Desdemona to show my mother how to look asleep.

He would then leave and return for the final scene, acting as Othello, while my mother lay breathing peacefully her last dramatic breath. The actual Othello, Artin, a handsome actor with a tremendous voice, who also sang with my mother in many operas and operettas, would watch Aram strangle Desdemona, and then try the part himself.

So many characters, on and off set, kept our home full of

life. To this day, I miss Vanda and Ida and her parents, as I do Barkev and Nersess.

Chapter 15

Using Men Like Pigs

A shrewd businesswoman, my mother was equally generous, hospitable, and, sometimes, extravagant. She amassed a small fortune by acting, dancing, and singing, and at times, in other, less public ways. For about ten years, she made her income from successful performances that brought us material comfort.

Both our bank account and our safety deposit box were stacked, she told me. At the time, I didn't know exactly what that meant, except that we were very comfortable and ate well. She never stopped reassuring me that we would never be short of food again. Her words still ring in my ears, for she repeated them often enough, in different ways. "All doors are open," was one of her sayings. Another was, "I use men like pigs; hogs, my darling. I ride them and pluck their bristles and make brushes out of them. I use them to the hilt, although they think they are using me."

She never stinted on anything. If, for instance, I needed a pair of shoes, down we would go to Harootyoon, our shoemaker, to order half a dozen pair of shoes, with handbags and belts to match. Harootyoon's shop was full of sharp carving knives with twisted, lethal shapes. An emaciated silhouette, he would bend over his sewing machine, intense, with calloused fingertips, sweating profusely in the airless place, surrounded by all sorts of calf, cow, and goat hides, dyes, well-thumbed magazines, as well as finished and unfinished shoes of all colors and sizes, hanging on the walls or resting on dusty shelves. The windowpanes were lined with strings and special needles with curved ends.

When our car drove up, he would look up from his work, and his paper-white face would break into a weak, tired grin. His leather apron, which inevitably would have a shoe in one of its many pockets, advanced before him. His hands, too, had a leathery look to them. The yellowish light that hung from the low ceiling emphasized the sweaty lines on his thin face. A toothless grin belied the youthful spark that still lingered in his fine, brown eyes. Harootyoon would lead us to the only two chairs available, with his usual deferential manner and always waited to sit behind his sewing-machine until after we were seated.

While my mother was served coffee, she asked about his wife and three children, as well as the state of his health. I would choose the shoe pattern, the leather, and the color from one of his many magazines. Then, Harootyoon would trace my foot size on a large piece of plain paper, a process that always tickled me, and my shoes would be ready within a week or two.

The magic of our visits to Harootyoon's shoe shop never became tarnished. His touching civility, his hospitality, and his honesty turned a simple occasion into an ennobling, human contact. We respected the love this artisan bore for his craft.

Like Harootyoon, my mother's jeweler, Karneek—also an Armenian—was a remarkable person. In his late-twenties, Karneek always wore his immaculate white shirt unbuttoned down to the last button but one, displaying, at the waist, a profusion of curly black hair. His arms were so hairy that the skin seemed covered with soft fur. He was also charming, and he would flash his perfect set of white, even teeth at the slightest opportunity, as a businessman might flash his card.

Karneek designed all of my mother's accessories, from diamond necklaces and rings, to watchbands and bracelets. With a few deft lines on a pad, he could draw designs of special beauty for my mother's approval. She kept Karneek busy enough for, at the time, she was hoarding gold sovereigns, and money was plentiful. I would watch my mother cover her arms, from wrist to elbow, with gold bracelets, so that her white arms were weighted down with solid gold. She told me that there was more where those came from. "Unfortunately," she said, chuckling wickedly, "I only have two arms." Each gold sovereign, I well recall, was encased in a solid gold case and attached to the next one with gold chains.

Chapter 16

A Salad of Nationalities

My mother was born in 1907, in Adana, Turkey, which meant she grew up during the time of the Armenian Genocide—the systematic mass murder and expulsion of ethnic Armenians in Turkey, carried out by the Ottoman Empire.

When my mother launched onto the subject of Armenia and Armenians, she would talk about her history and how it had not really affected her own parents. My interest in Armenian history was linked to my mother's own connection with it, and with her safety, which, to my child's mind, was of the utmost importance. It was hard for me to grasp the significance of such a vast tragedy, but when I enquired about the reasons for such destruction, she merely said that it was "dirty politics," that men were like "pawns" in the hands of various prominent powers of the day. In many countries, she explained, people lived peaceful lives—even people of different creeds—but where she had lived as a young girl, strong invaders caused rifts between people, keeping them weak in order to better control them. Divide and rule, she told me, was the credo, and it was all dirty politics.

In spite of, or perhaps because of, these opinions, my mother spoke Turkish with me and wanted me to learn Turkish, Armenian, and English. Not many people spoke English where we lived—not until the British invaded parts of the Middle East in 1941. After the British occupied our part of the Middle East, my mother told me that English was going to be the most important language in the world. But up until this point, Syria was under French mandate, and French was the language I spoke at the orphanage and the language of most people.

My mother hired a teacher to teach me Turkish. He was a wonderful gentleman who was born in Turkey, of Jewish faith. Both my mother and I enjoyed his visits over the course of several months. He was the one who told me that the Arabic alphabet was used by the Turks and that, later, Kemal Atatürk modernized the alphabet by replacing it with the Latin alphabet, like A, B, C, D. He also explained that the cedilla and the umlaut were borrowed. Also, he said that both Arabic and Hebrew are written from right to left and that modern Turkish is written, for instance, from left to right as in English and French.

I loved learning languages. Unfortunately, Turkish was not taught at the local schools, but Arabic was taught at the Lycée Français, where I was fortunate to have another wonderful gentleman teacher who explained everything so well. My mother and I spoke Turkish at home. If I did not know a word, I would point to it and ask in French what it was in Turkish and she would translate it for me. I progressed with time, and Turkish became our means of communication, except when we had visitors of different backgrounds. This salad of nationalities enhanced my love of language, literature, and music.

Chapter 17

She Must Take After Her Father

On Friday afternoons, some of the Turkish baths opened their doors to women. When my mother went, she was pampered and treated like a dignitary. There, the washerwoman would pour water from a wide basin over her white body with a huge copper ladle.

It was there that I first became aware of the scars of the knife wounds inflicted on her back by my father years earlier. I could see her wounds from where I stood. I imagined them to be fish swimming upstream because they shone so from certain angles. The axe wounds, too, were visible, but only when the woman shampooed her hair. It formed some kind of an irregular 'X' on the top of her head.

I did not enjoy the Turkish baths myself. I disliked the place with its Arabesque carvings on the lintel of the door, which gave access to the main entrance, and the domed rooms stuffed with what appeared to me to be the bottoms of green bottles. I hated the kassa, a black glove of coarse material used by Aliya, the emaciated attendant with a loincloth. She wore it like a mitten, painstakingly scrubbing every inch of my mother's body over and over again, pouring her entire concentration and energy into the process. The loose grayish skin rolled off my mother's body like a worm, cast and dropped on to the steaming marble floors of the baths to be carried along with soiled soapy water right into the troughs by our feet.

The raised dais, divided into cubicles with low partitions, attracted the local women swathed in multi-folded, embroidered heavy robes. Veils, skirts, and sandals came off to display a variety of bodies ready to be pummeled, pumice-stoned, and powdered. Steam and sweat filled every crevice. I dreaded my turn; I did not possess my mother's remarkable stamina.

The scene that fascinated me the most concerned a group of women, all with their backs to the others, facing the troughs, attempting to get rid of their pubic hair. The handful of regulars squatted, naked, performing their weekly duties indifferent to my own curious presence. I stood quite mesmerized by the tremendous tufts of curly hair being carried along the canals or troughs, bubbling with soiled soapy water. I watched the bits and pieces of floating, discarded human hair, fascinated by the speed with which they were carried along. Many years later, when I would watch children launching tiny boats by some water's edge, I would be reminded of that weird scene with the same remarkable, innocent fascination with which I watched the clumps of discarded hair floating by.

Aliya possessed most unusual breasts. They were dry, like two bits of hard, uneven rock which seem to have struck her bony chest and painfully stuck there. When Aliya finally finished with my mother, she wrapped her up in a colossal towel (as one would a baby), raised her feet, slipped them into the tall wooden clogs (which rose about ten inches above the ground to allow the soiled waters of the bath to flow under them), and led her to a canopied divan in an alcove of some sort. There, my mother sat and ate peeled, skinned orange segments prepared for her, and drank rose water, which was supposed to be good for the heart.

Shortly after I'd returned home from the orphanage and my mother began taking me with her to the Turkish baths, I heard Aliya ask my mother, as if I was not even there, "Who is this dark, ugly, skinny, hairy child you bring with you now?" My mother replied, casually, that I was her daughter, and that she had finally managed to take me out of the orphanage.

"She doesn't look a bit like you, Madame. You are so fair-skinned and lovely and plump and hairless. You have such beautiful smooth skin."

Aliya looked at me once again and back at my mother and added, "She must take after her father." And again, casually, my mother responded by saying, "Yes, that is the case."

Aliya rarely treated me with the gentleness and consideration she demonstrated towards my mother. Instead, she treated my hair and my body the way an angry baker might knead tough dough. She slapped the black, glove-like, grainy cloth over my frail frame until I turned the color of a lobster, and she didn't really wash my hair. She took out all her frustrations by tugging at its roots by the handful, working the lather to a frenzy, hardly allowing me time to take a breath in between rinses. She once revived me by pouring ice cold, running water over my burning body. Her wiry fingers traveled over my aching skull in an aggressive manner I have rarely encountered since.

To give the woman her due, she always ensured that I was well scrubbed, even if parts of my skin and hair were left behind in her two capable hands. My terror of the fierce, dried-up lady kept me from making the slightest gesture of defiance, for I knew that my head and body were at her mercy, at least once a week.

Eventually, the time came when it was clear I could no longer stand her treatment in the steaming salons of the Turkish baths: I fainted from the pain. That persuaded my mother to have a shower installed at home especially for me.

Chapter 18

Identical Dresses

My mother spoiled me, and that might have changed me into an unreasonable monster except that her sense of equity kept that tendency in check. I did not realize this lesson until the day she came to the door of her bedroom, which adjoined the living room, to hear what I was shouting. I remember every word she said on that occasion, for the simple reason that my mother rendered it unforgettable. I also remember that she was wearing a yellow dress I had never seen before. It was very becoming. She had come to seek my approval.

I was shouting at our servant's younger daughter, Anush, as my mother stood by, listening, "You are nobody! You are not even a servant. You are just a servant's daughter! You and your mother must do everything we order you to do. Otherwise, you would both starve! Now, go and polish my new shoes!"

My mother stood motionless. It took her a minute or two to relax the stern look on her face. Finally, she managed to smile as if she were acting and said, "My love, we all know how important you are. Please explain to me what you just said to her. I missed the beginning."

The poor girl was crying. I looked her up and down with disdain. Her clothes were old and her shoes were well worn, but her hair was clean and parted in the middle and braided on each side. She was older than I was, but I could not say by how many years. So, I obliged my mother by replying in a haughty manner. "Some people," I began, "like us, are rich, and others, like her and her mother, are nothing. So we look after them. We are important, and they are our servants. I just asked her to polish my shoes, Maman, and she refused to do it. We did everything for the rich girls at the orphanage."

My mother nodded, which I took for a sign of approval. After a long silence, while the girl sniffled and blew her nose as quietly as she could, my mother told us that she had come to show us her new yellow dance costume. I expressed my approval, for she did look lovely in it, with her thick auburn hair cascading down her white shoulders and catching the sun. And that particular yellow became her well.

She then enquired whether I would like to go shopping at a place called the Bon Marché. "I want to buy you some material for a dress, darling," she explained.

I was overjoyed. I threw my arms around her neck and kissed her. The girl stood there, not knowing what to do. She was too hurt to say a word. My mother then turned to Anush. "You are to come with us."

At the Bon Marché, we searched through bolts of cloth until I finally saw a red color I thought I would like. My mother then ordered a quantity of the red cloth and asked the salesman to cut another length of the same but with an extra meter for good measure.

Anush remained silent as we went back out to the car and while we drove to our dressmaker's house, located at the other end of the city. We had to leave the car some distance away because the street was too narrow to be driven through. We walked over old Roman roads, where people on opposite sides of the street could practically shake hands through their upstairs apartment windows.

At Charlotte's, my mother lifted the latch, pushing open the wide, low wooden front door, and in we went. The open courtyard, surrounded by high walls, at the center of which stood a water well with its pail dangling in mid-air, at the end of a thick, wet rope, enclosed a small house of three or four rooms.

Charlotte sat peacefully sewing under a shady lattice, beside a woven trellis of hanging vines laden with deep purple grapes. When she saw my mother, she got up to greet her, at the same time shouting instructions to her mother in the kitchen to prepare some Turkish coffee and some lemonade. For some reason, our dressmaker's thick ankles never failed to catch my attention. Like our servant, Marie, she moved stiffly, with obvious difficulty.

After the normal exchange of small talk, my mother handed Charlotte the package and opened a fashion magazine so that I might pick out the pattern I liked. When our dressmaker commented on the extra piece in the package, my mother simply explained that she was ordering two dresses of the same pattern, not one. The second dress, I realized with a feeling of shame, was for Anush. Charlotte took our measurements, we ate a few biscuits, drank the delicious lemonade, answered a few questions asked by Charlotte and her mother, and then we left.

When the dresses were ready, after a few fittings, my mother asked both of us to keep them on while we drove from our dressmaker's house to the Diana Studios to see Ruba, her personal photographer and publicity agent.

Ruba seated Anush beside me on a low bench and moved a set of portable garden scenery behind us, placing two Roman columns at each end of the bench into the foreground. Then he walked backwards, his eyes still on us, opened the skylight, then disappeared under the black cloth, and told us both to smile.

My mother did not move from the armchair opposite us. She said not a word and made not the slightest attempt to console me. All she said, when the photograph was finally taken in living color, was that we both looked lovely in red.

As promised, the photograph was ready within a week. It had been enlarged and framed, and was in color, as ordered. It hung over my bed for years. My mother never once commented on my poor behavior regarding that episode with Anush. She literally let the picture speak a thousand words. I never forgot that lesson.

Chapter 19

Breaking Cups

I soon learned that my mother was unlike other mothers. One day, while sipping Turkish coffee one afternoon with her friend, Nevart, my mother asked Marie to bring in the rest of the fine china set. I was sitting watching. It was a fine afternoon, and, for a change, there was a breeze moderating the heat.

"Nevart! Nevart! Listen to the sound of this demitasse as I throw it against that wall, over there," said my mother. She then threw all the demitasses, one by one, shrieking with pleasure at the sound each made as it went dashing and splintering into pieces.

Nevart, not in the least bit amused, told my mother that she was crazy. But this only made her laugh even more loudly. She told her friend it was wonderful to see a fragile bit of china dash against a solid object like a wall, that people were afraid to break china because it was so delicate, and yet it was because it was so delicate that it made such a wonderful sound when it crashed.

Ever the outspoken person that she was, Nevart told my mother that it was a terrible waste of money, but my mother argued that she was in a position to afford to waste it, and that, in itself, was a reward. Nonetheless, my mother accepted her friend's honesty graciously and cheerfully enough.

It could be that the sound of china breaking was, in some way, related to my mother's love of music, of sound itself, which would include the sound of words. At times, she would call me in, to hear her read out a passage she found beautiful. The right choice of words she called, "spoken music." She often read to me, but in her own strange way—she would read everything, including the punctuation marks. For instance, if she were reading Hamlet's soliloquy, she would say, "to be or not to be, semi-colon." And then, "that is the question, period," and so on.

At other times, she would recite a long poem by heart, stopping only to ask me which of the words I thought were the most beautiful and why. She, in turn, would jot down her own list, and then we would compare them.

Chapter 20

A Poor Family

Our life together had its own kind of regularity. At rare times when she was up early for some reason, she always joined me for breakfast as well as for lunch, and she would ask Marie to join us at the table. Marie would invariably decline with a touching humility. But my mother would not go along. She would insist that Marie was as great and as wonderful, if not more wonderful, than most of her guests, that we were all sisters under the skin, and that it was due to the damned circumstances of her life that she often found herself acting the prima donna on and off the stage.

She told me over and over again that, in this cock-eyed world, people care less about honest, hard-working people than the affluent who exploit them, that we are far too impressed by appearances rather than by character and noble deeds. "What have I to offer, Marie, my dear, is a pound of flesh, whereas you are offering your daily energy for a pittance. It is a poor exchange, a shameful barter, Marie, believe me, but there we are: nowhere really. Come please eat. Let me serve you for a change."

I will never forget Marie's lovely, wrinkled face, her mild, honey-colored eyes, her full gentle mouth. Her whole demeanor spoke of a noble humility, a cheerful resignation to the life she had to lead.

When my mother was away on tours, Marie stayed a little longer with me so that I would not be alone in the big house. I was busy enough during the day, for I read a great deal and spent some time in calisthenics and every morning before breakfast I did exercises—I lifted weights or went cycling—but I was often lonely when I saw that Marie was about to leave, after she served me my supper and had cleared the table. I often wished that Marie and her daughters would spend the night with me, but I never dared ask.

One evening, however, just as she was getting ready to leave, I ran after her to the door and asked her to take me with her. At first she hesitated with her usual kind smile. She explained as gently as she could that her house was not in a state acceptable to me, that it was very, very small, and that I would not like it. She said they had so little furniture that most of them slept on the floor.

But when I persisted, she finally gave way and we set out on an interminable walk through dark, narrow lanes. Until then I had not realized the poor woman walked that long route, twice a day, in order to earn a miserable thirty pounds a month.

She lived at the top of a flight of steep stone stairs. There was no railing, so I climbed up by touching the wall to my left. It was so dark; I felt that one false step could land me on the stone courtyard below.

The first thing I saw was Anush seated on a low divan with an eastern rug under her, reading by an oil lamp, while her elder sister sewed a blouse.

Marie explained I was to spend the night with them because I felt a little lonely. They looked pleased. The elder sister put down the blouse to come and shake hands with me, and Anush got up immediately after closing her book; I detected no hard feelings on her part about the photograph we had taken together in identical red dresses.

Marie's tiny mother, toothless and almost blind, emerged from the kitchen, smiling a gummy smile, saying what a surprise and an honor it was to welcome me to her house.

They were running around me, offering me drink and food, suggesting a game of cards, and laying out the phonograph records. Anush, who made room for me beside her on the couch, showed me the book she had been reading, written in a language I was yet to learn. She was proud of the fact that she could read English.

In vain, I tried to decipher the strange new language. I pointed to a word enquiring about its meaning. She explained that it was the name of the author, perhaps one of the best in the world; it was *Huckleberry Finn*, and the author was a man named Mark Twain and that his real name was Samuel Langhorne Clemens. It surprised me that my mother had not mentioned Mark Twain to me, nor read from his book. The first book she ever read to me from cover to cover was *The Wandering Jew*.

I felt a new kind of respect for the girl as I handed the book back to her. She promised to teach me how to count up to ten in English after supper, if I so desired. I said I would be happy to learn to do that.

We all sat around the rickety table covered with a plastic tablecloth, with a vase of artificial roses at its center. In one corner of the small room stood a double-size mattress rolled up like a Swiss roll, standing on its end. The soup bowls were all of different sizes. Marie's mother placed a huge container of lentil soup near the vase, handing each one of us a tablespoon, and we each took turns dipping into it and filling up our respective bowls. There was bread, freshly baked by the old lady, rolled vine leaves called sarma, with lemon juice squeezed over them, and a dessert of baklava made with butter, honey, and nuts.

I kept thinking how wonderful it was to be there. I was overwhelmed by the sheer joy of being with Marie and her family. My feet rested on the bare cement floor. It felt lovely and cool underfoot. Everyone was enjoying the food, but I knew no one did as much as I.

After they cleared the table and washed the dishes, we played cards and listened to some records in different languages. Towards midnight, the great fat mattress was unrolled on the bare floor to make the communal bed I was to share with Marie's daughters. Marie's place was on the divan where Anush had been sitting when we first arrived that evening, and the grandmother slept on the divan by the kitchen entrance.

The lamp was lowered after one of the girls pointed to the chamber-pot by the kitchen entrance—they had no other toilet—and the elder of the two put up with our chatter in bed while I was being taught the cardinal numerals up to ten, going over them patiently, again and again.

When the sun woke me up, I found myself lying alone on a large mattress. Everyone was up and about, but I was told to go back to sleep, not to hurry, that there was nowhere to go that day. But I was far too happy to sleep. I got up, brushed my teeth, and packed my pajamas.

Marie took the porcelain basin in which I had washed my face and threw its content over the wall into the courtyard below. It did not feel particularly safe because the wall behind us consisted merely of a plastic sheet. As I stepped back, she smiled at me. It was not a smile of courtesy or a shield behind which some might need to hide either her dishonesty or sorrow. Nor was it a smile of gratitude. It was a smile full of genuine affection.

And it was at Marie's that I saw my first scorpion. With its deadly tail in the air, it came out of the cracks, walking towards us. I did not recognize it. It was the elder sister who saw it first and told me to watch out. She warned me not to touch it explaining that it was poisonous. She then got a stone from the kitchen and flattened it at once.

There was no shortage of stones there. The kitchen roof itself was held down with huge stones and bits of corrugated tin, forming a strange patchwork overhead. The gray walls were covered with rotting plaster. The whole house was composed of a room and a half, with the three-walled kitchen, and the plastic fourth wall which overlooked the courtyard.

It was a poor family's house, yet I can say that I never went anywhere else during my childhood where I saw more genuinely hospitable people. All too soon came the time for my departure. I was concerned that I had already overstayed my visit, but I wanted so much to stay yet another night. I was, however, saved the embarrassment when both girls, almost in the same breath, begged me to stay another night.

Altogether, I stayed two nights at our servant's house with her two wonderful daughters and their grandmother. Before the end of the second day, I set out to buy a French record that was popular in those days. When the table was set for my last meal with them, I felt particularly pleased with myself that I had, in some small way, shown my gratitude towards the wonderful family. But, alas, when I went to occupy my usual place at the table, I heard a sharp crack. I had sat on the record.

The next morning, the grandmother was still in bed while we were all up and about. It was Marie who first discovered her mother's death. She must have whispered it to her daughters, for, just as I was packing my things, ready to leave, Marie's elder daughter told me that her grandmother had died in her sleep. I went to see the old lady lying on her back on the divan. She lay as stiff as a board, her bony, wrinkled hands joined on her chest, her sunken eyes closed, her hollow cheeks waxen, and her toothless mouth half open. It was my first brush with someone's death. We were all in a state of shock. No one wailed or cried.

After saying goodbye to Marie and her daughters, I made my way back home as the sun rose high in the eastern sky. My feet started slowly but before I knew it, I was running.

Back home, I ran towards my mother with open arms. She had just returned from another successful tour. She was glowing with joy. She looked fresh and happy in a bright red velour dress, with the skirt unevenly cut all around just below the knee in strange triangles. She was wearing a turban of some kind and red, high-heeled shoes buckled elegantly over her high instep.

For pure showmanship, she was sporting a pince-nez, which she removed with a theatrical gesture and gave me a hug before ordering me to open one of the trunks. I was accustomed to seeing her surrounded by trunks and suitcases full of surprises, but I never expected such a large one. She looked so happy, so proud of herself.

I lifted the heavy lid slowly, my mind flying back to that day at the orphanage when she had come to see me for the first time with a suitcase full of treats. But this time I marveled at the presents. There was a pretty little pink fan with three propellers. The fan could be wound like a clock and it could run for about an hour while blowing a sweet scent into the air. There were a few books, including Bernardin de Saint-Pierre's *Paul et Virginie*, and boxes of Perugina candies and special French biscuits and a roll of pictures of movie stars I had never seen or heard of before—names like Myrna Loy, Chester Morris, Freddie Bartholomew, and Harold Lloyd.

When I went to bed that night, I unrolled the pictures and stared with adoration at the faces, then I rolled them up again and propped them up beside the dictionaries on my bookshelf. Above, hung the humiliating photograph of Anush and myself in our bright red dresses. I sat and stared at it for a long time before falling asleep.

Chapter 21

The Other Side

After having spent an enjoyable weekend at Marie's house and having returned home to my mother's warm embrace and her marvelous gifts, I was ready to return to school that Monday morning. As usual, I had my breakfast alone and after that, I was driven to the Franciscan School where I had been sharing my education with the wealthy girls. Now that I was on the other side of the fence, so to speak, I sat side by side with the daughters of wealthy families. I could play tennis, dressed in white shorts, if I so desired.

The nuns, whose Janus faces I had observed from both sides of the orphanage, had been my teachers and tormentors. I had taken orders from them every waking minute of the day for many years. Now they complied with my slightest wish, for they were being amply paid. We were the financial backers of the institution on which they depended.

I had spent years in the hallowed halls of the Franciscan orphanage and had been deprived of a good education because I was poor. Even though my mother read passages from well-known works of literature to me, and I saw many operas and other theatrical productions, my education was still limited. I had to work hard in order to catch up and even try to surpass the other students.

I started taking piano lessons in the basement with the rich girls. Within a few months, I was given the privilege of taking my piano lessons in the salon where only cardinals and other dignitaries were received. Later that year, when I was awarded a gold medal for my achievements at the piano, it seemed ironic that the same Mother Superior who had made me wear the sign, "Je suis une fille désobéissante," was the person who handed me my prize before the whole school assembly.

However, that brief moment of glory did not make me many friends among my fellow students who knew that I had been an orphan on the other side, and my mother's reputation was nothing to boast about. Perhaps they knew or suspected that some of their own fathers had paid her clandestine visits, much to the embarrassment of their own respectable mothers.

Often, I had to fall back on my own resources, trying to teach myself Morse Code, for instance, or reading, studying, or cycling on a rented tricycle at the price of one franc an hour because I had no real friends there. One of my mother's loyal friends helped me a great deal with French grammar, and I am still grateful to him, today.

Lacking school friends, in a sense, gave me a new kind of freedom. I had ample time to study anything I liked or for physical exercises. I felt immediate release from physical restraint every time I went for a bicycle ride on my own. I would pedal furiously, my heart thumping with excitement.

One day, I wondered what it would be like if I could cycle to the orphanage and take Josephine, Number 72, home because my mother told me that Madame Flora did not live too far from where we lived. But as a day student on the rich girls' side, I was not permitted to speak to any of the orphans.

I missed Josephine and I wondered if, in some way, I could free her from that awful place, even for an afternoon, and have her come to our house for a visit. It was a crazy idea, but to me, as a naïve child, it seemed so simple. The bar at the back of the tricycle would take her weight, and she could hang on to me for support while I pedaled; since I had been driven to the school back and forth several times a day, I felt I knew the route well.

I took the plunge one day when my mother was performing at an old local movie house that had been recently converted into a theatre. I rented the tricycle for only one hour; I intended on returning it as soon as I had set Josephine free from those depressing surroundings. Instead of returning the tricycle to its owner that same day, I took it home just before dark, while my mother was still at the theatre, and made sure that Marie was still in the kitchen. I carried it into the house and hid it under my bed. The embroidered borders of the satin covers reached to the floor, so there was no problem of detection. There still remained the question of taking the tricycle out the following day to get Josephine, but if I brought it in, I could surely take it out, I thought to myself confidently, and with a touch of childish pride. I was in no rush to execute my plan. I had the tricycle, and I was at home on holiday, but I must have waited a little too long.

On the second day, three men appeared at our door, demanding to see my mother. Marie called her while I stood watching, having no idea who they were. My mother came into the waiting room in her magnificent housecoat, looking somewhat puzzled and perhaps a little disgruntled, for no one dared wake her that early in the morning. Suddenly, one of the men shouted, "That's her! That's the girl who stole the tricycle! That's her!"

I stood as far back as I could, wishing I could disappear from the face of the earth. I was terrified of the angry man who was shouting and pointing at me. His expression so resembled that of the man at the marketplace years earlier that I could almost feel the cobblestone street coming up to meet me. I forgot I was at home, standing on the Italian marble floor, with Marie, our cook, and Elias listening to every word.

"Just a moment, sir," my mother said, "do I understand correctly that my little girl borrowed a tricycle from your shop and failed to return it?"

"She did!" the man replied, "She stole one of our four tricycles in broad daylight yesterday!"

My mother turned to reassure me, saying, "Darling, darling, don't be afraid. But please tell me, is it true that you did rent a tricycle two days ago?"

It was one of the worst days of my life, I think. How could I lie? I had never lied to anyone, let alone to my mother. But I felt I had no other choice. So I said, "No, Maman, I never did."

"She's lying!" the man shouted outraged. He then asked my mother, "Why don't you let these policemen search the house?"

That was when my mother raised her authoritative voice for the first time. "My daughter never lies!" she said, and turned to me once again, her voice full of patience, "Darling, did you or did you not borrow a tricycle from this gentleman's shop? Tell me."

Something stronger than myself made me say, "No, Maman."

"That is enough for me," my mother then told the men, "Gentlemen, you must have the wrong house. Please leave."

The owner of the tricycle gesticulated wildly shouting, "I'm not leaving without the tricycle! We're going to search the house, Madame."

Without flinching, my mother said, "Not without a warrant, gentlemen," and, turning to Marie, said, in the same cool voice, "Marie, please show these gentlemen to the door. Good day to you, gentlemen."

The men turned on their heels and left, but they were back that same afternoon with a warrant to search the house. Marie and Elias looked puzzled by the strange turn of events, but most of all, my mother was aggrieved. She followed the policemen from room to room, making gratuitous comments on the futility of such an action, that they would regret it, and so on, when much to my dismay and horror, they opened my bedroom door, went in, and lifted up the satin cover draped around my bed. I thought I would die.

My mother was dreadfully embarrassed, and as she followed the men out, she offered to make amends and pay for any inconvenience. She then ordered Marie to keep me in my room without lunch or dinner.

I sat in my little armchair by the balcony watching traffic, my eyes smarting. I was so ashamed of myself, I kept wondering if my mother would ever come in and talk to me. Lunchtime passed. No one came to see me. I waited for hours, and when the sun began to set abruptly, as it did in that part of the world, I put the lights on, cursing myself and wondering what to do, when Marie walked in, carrying a tray of food. She said that my mother did not know anything about it, so I should eat quickly so that she could take the tray back before my mother returned.

I wolfed down the delicious food in spite of my feelings of deep guilt. Marie gave me a wet serviette, one corner of which was soapy. I wiped my mouth and fingers and returned it to her. I waited for her to say something about the terrible incident, but she simply took the tray and left, closing the door behind her.

I felt like a prisoner. I could not help calling to mind the dungeon-like basement of the orphanage where Josephine and I had been deprived of food and drinks. My heart trembled when my mother finally came in later that evening. She had the same set expression on her face. She looked at me and sat on my bed facing me. She said, "Why, darling, why did you not return the tricycle? And why didn't you tell me about it? You know I can buy you a tricycle, if you only ask for it."

A floodgate of tears opened. My nose was running all over my lips and chin and down my pajamas. She produced a white linen handkerchief from the pocket of her robe, the one with the hand-painted peacocks on each side of the front flap. She avoided looking straight into my eyes, though she proceeded to wipe mine gently and lovingly. She waited for me to say something.

Close to breaking down, I explained to my mother that I wanted to go and bring Josephine home from the orphanage, and that I had fully intended to return the tricycle after getting Josephine out.

After what seemed ages, she enquired how, exactly, was I going to manage to take Josephine out of the orphanage.

"I don't know, Maman," I muttered between sobs, "maybe hide in the bushes somewhere near the big doors, leave the tricycle there, and go and ask to speak to her for a few minutes and then run away together as we had tried to do before."

It was at that moment that my mother's honey hazel eyes met mine. Her expression mellowed considerably. She wanted to know did I intend to warn her grandmother before undertaking such an adventure.

I shook my head.

"Why, darling?"

I shrugged my shoulders helplessly.

"I was told by one of the sisters that you had tried to run away together and that you had been punished for it," she said calmly. "I would have done the same thing myself, but don't you realize, sweetheart, that borrowing a tricycle for one franc an hour under false pretenses is called stealing?"

I explained that I had intended to return it, eventually. But she said, "Yes, but does that justify the theft?"

I felt helpless. She gathered her robe. "Are you hungry, sweetheart?" she asked.

I wanted to tell her that Marie had fed me but I was afraid. All I could say was, "No, Maman."

It was on the following day that my mother told me that it was under her strict orders that I had been clandestinely fed.

And that was when she used one of her memorable sayings, "Remember, darling, frighten the dog, but don't beat him." She took me in her arms and kissed me.

Chapter 22

A Man's World

Shortly after the tricycle incident, my mother took me to Josephine's mother's house where she lived with her other daughter, Mariam. It was spotless. They had their meals in the basement at a large table covered with a handmade cloth. We were greeted with great warmth. Josephine's mother, I found out then, worked as a part-time house cleaner. When she walked and talked, she breathed heavily and audibly as if in constant pain.

Josephine's sister, Mariam, who appeared old enough to be her mother, resembled what I imagined Helen of Troy would have looked like. She was a golden-haired, blue-eyed, straight-nosed, fair-complexioned woman, with a smooth, high forehead. She was unusually tall for a woman born in that country and she was thickset, with huge shoulders and well-shaped legs. There was a regal aloofness about her presence. She did not seem to belong in that house, nor in that country, for that matter. Yet, if I imagined her to be Greek, in the old sense of the word, she truly belonged in a gold-dome palace, surrounded by servants, fanning her, and feeding her grapes. She could have been related to my mother, rather than to Madame Flora or Josephine, who was dark, skinny, and hairy like me...quite unlike her elder sister.

During our visit, my mother took out an envelope from her purse and handed it to Madame Flora. She apologized that it was only a small amount, but she hoped that it would assist them in some way. It was dirty money, my mother told the old lady, winking and smiling mischievously. She also told her not to hesitate to call on her any time she needed help.

Madame Flora put her podgy arms around my mother and kissed her on both cheeks, wheezing, while droplets escaped from the corners of her closed eyes. When she recovered, she told my mother that she had read Mariam's Turkish coffee cup earlier that day and had told her that there was some money coming into their house from somewhere. She admitted that the times were hard. "My knees hurt and I can't do as much cleaning as I used to. I'm getting old and useless. Mariam gets the odd customer, but they don't pay her as much as they used to. You are a big-hearted woman, Madame, very big-hearted. Thank you."

The woman looked pathetically at my mother, while still wiping her eyes and trying to smile at the same time. Mariam watched us all sitting upright, her back to the wall, her blue eyes reflecting cool, superior objectivity. I took it all in, sitting on a chair beside my mother and feeling proud of her.

Finally, when my mother mentioned Josephine and getting her out of the orphanage, Madame Flora wondered what Josephine would do if she did come out. They could hardly manage to eat twice a day as it was, and she knew that she could not afford to send Josephine to school, nor could her sister.

"Mariam is beautiful like you, Madame. Men like her looks. But what chance does Josephine stand? Look at Mariam. I have a few more years perhaps, and then, what will happen to Mariam? She cannot read or write. We were always too poor to attend school. I was lucky to get married, but my husband died and I was left with my child, Mariam, and I worked hard to help her by doing some cleaning and ironing and mending clothes. When Mariam was ready to go to school, we had no money because schools, Madame, as you know, cost the earth. So she never learned how to read and write. And no one asked for her hand in marriage. She was not lucky, although she is good looking. There are no woman doctors, lawyers, architects, teachers, dentists, and so on. There are many midwives, but they had to learn the skills. There are no waitresses, as some people told us, as in Europe or the United States, going by the movies that they had seen. So I am told. I know nothing. The only work a poor woman can do is to become a servant or a cook in a house, or like Mariam, get the odd customer so that we can survive. She tried to clean houses but men always wanted to sleep with her. I don't know what is to become of us, Madame. I really don't know." She shook her head, rubbing her fat, calloused hands together.

Then Mariam spoke up. "If Josephine comes home, she'll end up like me, on her back, with anyone who'll pay. She won't be able to go out with friends without being called a whore, but the rich, married woman who has a lover or two, is still respected, whereas Josephine will be branded for life. Men can do anything they want. We are to stay home and just be available. That's what she'll have to face. Not a pretty prospect, I say." Mariam spoke with unusual detachment. There was little emotion in her voice, unlike Madame Flora's. "And, unlike you, Madame, I have no education. You can read and write and act and sing. I am told that you have a beautiful voice. Everybody loves you."

After some more Turkish coffee for my mother and the usual orange juice for me, Madame Flora became more optimistic. She said, "Perhaps Josephine should stay at the orphanage and become a nun. After all, nuns don't work that hard for their living, not in the real sense of the word, and they spend their days in prayer and telling the orphans what to do and of course they also teach. They drink the best wines, wear the cleanest clothes, they always have a rent-free place in which to live, and people respect them because they are good and they pray most of the time. Of course, Josephine has to show some interest in it, otherwise, she will have to go and work at some rich family's house when she is too old to stay at the orphanage. I don't know what can be done, Madame. We can do our best. That's all."

"Who knows," my mother sighed putting her jacket on and taking my hand, "things change. They might change for the better. I saw a Turkish girl at the cash desk at the Cinema a few days ago. She was a lovely young girl. She said she had applied for the job and got it. Maybe by the time Josephine is out, she will get some kind of work that, until now, only men do."

We left Madame Flora's house, and when we arrived home, my mother told me that she would do anything she could to help Josephine and her sister and mother, but that I came first. She said she wanted me to finish my studies and then learn English, which was taught only at The American Missionary School in the city, and that she would send me to Geneva to study law. That was her dream for me. "I want you to get out of this mess, darling. I will have to concentrate on you first and foremost. Josephine's fate is uncertain, like most women here, but I can't afford to worry about her. Remember, I am ready to do anything to save you. You must remain as pure as you are. I will sell my soul to the devil to see you succeed in this crazy world. Just ask me for anything, and I will do my utmost to provide it for you. My life is finished in a sense. I will do anything for your safety and for your success."

Chapter 23

Christina

A few days after we visited with Josephine's family, when my mother was back from the theatre at around two o'clock in the morning, there came a sharp knock on our front door. I was ready to run and open it, but my mother shouted for me to stop, for she knew she was not expecting any visitors at that late hour. She put on her housecoat and went to her bedroom to pick up the automatic Browning revolver she kept under her pillow. She returned with it in her right-hand pocket. She told me to keep away from the door and, having turned on all the lights, she went to open it. My mother had demonstrated the use of the gun to me at one time, saying, "If you release this safety catch, darling, you aim to kill. We need it because we are alone in this alien world." She had let me hold it for a second. It felt light enough, but its power terrified me. I gave it back to her, shrinking from it as one would from a cobra.

No sooner was the door open, that a young woman threw herself at my mother's feet, sobbing and begging for her help. My mother pointed to the couch and asked the stranger to calm down and to sit down. I stood in the corner of the room by the hydrangea plant, startled by the unexpected visitor and her agitated state.

My mother pulled her up by the hand. "Get up, please. Sit down and tell me why you're here." She then closed the front door. The woman sat. She was sobbing uncontrollably. I felt sorry for the woman. I did not know what to do. My mother went to the kitchen and came back with a tray of food and some coffee. They then sat side by side, taking a sip or two in complete silence as though each was gathering her thoughts.

My mother spoke up, “Tell me what’s bothering you.”

Tearful and hardly able to breathe, the woman told my mother that she had escaped from the local brothel that same morning, but, before going on, she stopped again to wipe her whole face that was dripping wet. She threw a furtive glance in my direction and asked if it was all right to talk in front of me. My mother gave her permission to do so by responding, “Of course it is all right. She can watch and learn but not imitate, as I keep telling her.” My mother tried to say it as lightly as she could.

She told us that her name was Christina and she had heard of my mother’s goodness. She had been sold to the brothel by her own husband. He had married her when she was only twelve years old. He was a pimp and received his cut according to the take. When Joseph, a young French sergeant, had come along, they fell in love and he asked her to marry him. Her husband would not let her go, and in any case, the authorities would not allow her to leave the country.

Christina explained that she had a plan and that her idea was to take a bus into the city, cross the frontier with other travelers where Joseph was being posted, and marry him there. She added that she had a ten-year-old daughter, named Jamilla, who was in the care of her grandmother.

My mother enquired where Joseph was. Christina replied that he was at the barracks, but that she was hoping to leave from the bus depot at four in the afternoon; that is, within a few hours, while Joseph was to make his own way to his new destination with the rest of the soldiers, which was about a few hours’ drive from where we were, and that they would meet in the new city and get married there. Once they were married, they would be allowed to go all the way to France, and, later, when things were safe, she would send for her daughter. My mother asked her why she was not taking Jamilla with her now. Christina replied that she feared what would happen to her child if they were caught together.

Christina was about to fall on her knees again when my mother stopped her. She must think, she said, she wanted to help the wretched woman, but the question was how? I could not help thinking that there was an ironic parallel between my wish to take Josephine, number 72, out of the orphanage and my mother's wish to help this woman's escape from the brothel.

After a long deliberation, my mother decided to help, and I was to be included in the plan. Christina was to remain hidden in our house until the bus was about to leave for that particular destination. If anybody were to call, they would be told that there was an ailing friend in my mother's bedroom. Marie would be given the day off, and Elias would be sent on a long errand.

My role was to go to the grandmother's house with one of Christina's artificial pearl earrings to prove who I was and then take Jamilla to a movie theatre and there, in the washroom, where we would both change into different clothing and come out wearing sunglasses. At the bus station, we were to buy two one-way tickets, and just before the bus line-up started moving, Christina would take my place and board the bus with her daughter. For my part, I was given a bag with two hats, two scarves, two pairs of dark sunglasses, a loose skirt with an elastic waist, and another with buttons all the way up the front. My mother advised me to tell Jamilla not to take off her clothes, but to simply wear the skirt over them. She tied the scarf around my chin and neck, pressed my face in both hands and kissed me on the cheek.

When morning came, I left home before Marie's arrival. I walked as fast as I could, but I avoided running and I kept walking in the shadows as much as possible. It took me about half an hour to reach Christina's mother's house. When the old lady opened the door, she looked somewhat nervous. A little girl's head appeared from behind the old lady's ample, black skirt. In the morning sunlight, they both looked anxious and glad to see me. The door was opened wide and immediately shut behind me.

She wished to know if I was the kind lady's daughter. I told her that I was and I handed her the pearl earring Christina had given me. She raised both hands and praised God for His mercy. She began to weep, burying her whole wrinkled face into a huge, soiled handkerchief. She kept thanking God, and, every so often, stroking the little girl's head gently, slowly, as if rubbing it with holy ointment.

Realizing the urgency of the situation, she turned to me, thanking me and my mother, over and over again, and got the little girl dressed up for the eventual trip, hugging and kissing her at least a dozen times, while still crying. Reluctantly, she handed me a small parcel containing some bread and cheese for Jamilla and her mother. "For the trip," she clarified. The old lady's face seemed to contain all the heartbreak in the world as she reached out to kiss her grandchild for the last time. She warned Jamilla to listen to everything Madame's daughter told her.

I can still see her waving her huge handkerchief as I took Jamilla firmly by the hand and walked away. By the time I arrived back home, Marie had been dismissed for the day with extra money and food for her daughters, and Elias had disappeared with a long list of things to purchase.

When Christina saw her daughter enter my mother's bedroom, she became hysterical. She insisted on kissing my mother's hand, saying what a wonderful woman she was, and how fortunate I was to have just such a mother. Then, before my mother and Christina disappeared into the bedroom to work on the disguise, Jamilla and I were sent off on our own new errand after having locked the front door.

The bus depot was a confusion of people and animals. The air was hot and dusty, people were shoving, children were screaming, goats were bleating, chickens were clucking in their cages on top of buses, geese were carried in open baskets, along with all sorts of vegetables. Men were sweating, impatient for the bus to start. Most of the people spoke Arabic, a few spoke Greek, Turkish, or Armenian. The women sat patiently in their long, black robes and veils, only their beautiful brown eyes exposed.

Dilapidated and dangerously overloaded, the bus groaned under its own weight, leaning to one side as if ready to topple. The bus driver was seated at the wheel like a king on a throne. Painfully, the bus came to a halt in a cloud of hot dust. I stood in the lineup waiting for the bus, keeping an eye on Jamilla who was right in front of me, waiting for Christina to make her appearance. My heart skipped a beat when a shabbily dressed woman who looked to be in her sixties elbowed her way into the line, coming between Jamilla and myself.

I almost yelled at her for pushing her way, but when I looked more closely and saw that it was Christina herself, with her brown hair touched up with powder and cream, adding years to her appearance, I felt much better. As the other passengers began to crowd into the bus, I allowed myself to be pushed against Jamilla, slipped my ticket into Christina's hand, and edged away. I did not dare wait for the bus to take off. With deliberate effort, I placed one foot in front of the other till I reached our house, my heart still thumping.

As soon as I entered the house, my mother and I heard a loud knock. My mother opened the front door and touched a finger to her lips, her eyes darting towards a shifty-eyed toad of a man in the vestibule, who was searching the area with his eyes rather than looking at my mother.

I could tell immediately that my mother was displeased.

He said his name was Sami and that he was there to enquire about a woman called Christina. When my mother pretended not to know the person, he replied with an ugly grin that the woman in question had escaped from a local brothel, and that he aimed to find her. He looked around as if expecting Christina to materialize any second. My mother wished the man good luck, which rather confused me. He scratched the middle of his oily, graying hair, biting his lip with a weird smirk.

He repeated his question. "Are you saying that you never saw Christina, Madame?"

With her best theatrical gesture, my mother, said, no, she had never seen such a person, and wondered why such a person would come to our house. Disappointed, the man took his leave with an audible sigh, but, just before my mother closed the door behind him, she asked why he was interested in the woman called Christina. He stopped dead in his tracks; he looked at her with mocking eyes as if not believing a word she told him. "I am her husband, Madame," he said.

It seemed ages before he left our house. The door had been closed on him for only a few minutes, when there came another persistent knock. This time it was a younger, thinner stranger, whose manner was deferential as he explained that he was a detective. He showed his credentials and explained that he had been hired to inquire about a prostitute by the name of Christina who had escaped from a local brothel.

With cool hospitality, my mother asked the man in and offered him some coffee, while she sat listening to what he had to say. After a thoughtful sip, the detective apologized to my mother telling her that it was his duty to investigate, that the last thing he wished to do was to cause her any trouble. He also expressed the opinion that Christina was seen entering our house, and that he would appreciate it if she could be of any assistance in locating the said person.

My mother said that she knew nothing except that, a certain Mr. Sami had just been to our house to enquire about the same woman, and that he had claimed to be her husband. All this time, she did not flinch; she stared at the man straight in the eye. She then turned to me, all innocence and light, to ask me whether anyone called Christina had called at our house while she was asleep, without her knowledge. I hesitated a second and caught on. I replied, "No, Maman."

Christina had been warned by my mother not to communicate with us, by any means, for at least a year. But, sometime later, we received a letter of thanks from her, postmarked Paris, together with a parcel containing a brass vase made in North Africa. The letter, written in French, overflowed with gratitude and joy, and was signed by Christina, Jamilla, and Joseph. I was given the vase to keep. I still have it.

As for the detective, he never did return to our house, but only because my mother knew the right people. She simply had him fired for daring to enter our house and for his assumption that a respectable lady, like herself, would harbor any thoughts of helping, or even being associated with, a refugee from a house of ill-repute. It was simply unthinkable.

Chapter 24

The Flea-Ridden Family

Not too long after Christina and Joseph were married, a family of nine members knocked on our door. My mother was at home, relaxing between shows, so she did not seem to mind letting them in, although it was early in the morning. I was revolted.

There stood before us nine filthy, flea-ridden people. The man told my mother, point blank, that he had no money and that he, his wife, and seven children had just arrived in the city. They had been told that Madame was hospitable and that she would never turn down a poor family in distress.

He asked if they could spend the night at our house. In fact, they seemed to take it for granted. They squatted on our living room floor, the children wide-eyed and snotty-nosed, the young parents in shabby, well-worn clothes.

I had heard stories about my mother's generosity. I stood wondering what she would do. She surveyed them as one would a disaster scene, then commanded that first, they must go and wash, and then she would serve them all the food they needed and give them enough cash to last them a week or two.

I was told to bring out some water and clean towels, while the man and his wife kept up a litany of blessings, wishing us peace and prosperity, forever and ever, with God's will. They were gentle and grateful people, and they took turns washing and drying themselves slowly and with dignity.

I gathered up the dirty towels, while my mother filled them

up with food, reassuring them that there was no pork being served and that they should eat heartily. By the time they left the next day, they had made quite a mess of our living room. Thanking us profusely, they took the money and walked out of our lives with my mother's blessings.

Marie could not believe her eyes when she arrived later that morning. The disorder was unbelievable. "All those children, seven of them," she kept repeating. "Where did they all come from, Madame?"

My mother gave Marie the following answer: "The spiritual powers of this universe sent them to us, Marie, my dear, to test our hearts."

Chapter 25

God's Water

One summer morning, my mother and I were driven to a health spa because she had heard that the sulphur baths were good for you, even though she was in excellent health and I was no longer the sickly, anemic child I used to be. We went for the experience, my mother explained.

I well remember my mother standing upright in deep water, with me clinging to her back with my arms around her neck. It was something like a square bathtub that could accommodate about thirty people, and deep enough for grown-ups to stand, shoulder-deep, in the water that was supposed to cure sores, rheumatism of the joints, and other ailments. I was listening to my mother talking to another young woman who was also carrying a small child on her back. Suddenly, the waving movement of the water caught me in the face, filling my mouth. The two mothers did not seem to realize that I was drowning, but, just in time, my mother heard me gagging and gasping for breath and my grip loosening around her neck. Immediately, she took me out of the huge communal tub and tried to calm me down, but I never managed to control my fear of water again.

When she showed her ticket of admittance and was about to return to the tub, she noticed that the dirty run-off water was pouring itself into tiny rivulets and runnels outside the main stone building at the back of the baths.

An old man, whose bare legs were covered with red, running

sores, was scooping up the dirty water, along with the grit and mud, in his huge, bony hands, and washing his sores with what he thought was a miraculous liquid.

Not too far from the old man, a woman sat cupping both hands and basting her infant's infected arms with the same dirty water. Something must have drawn my mother to that location, for she asked them why they were not washing themselves inside, where the water was sparkling clean. They told her that they could not afford the fee charged by the officials at the door. Without the slightest hesitation, my mother shepherded them to the door, guarded by two armed men in grubby uniforms with missing buttons and dirty old boots, who barred her way with their rifles.

Grabbing me by the hand tightly, she attempted to force her way into the baths with these people. Again the guards barred the way. Outraged, she shouted in their faces, "Don't you see that the water is contaminated out there? Can't you smell the urine? Don't you realize that the sores these people have will become infected?"

They stolidly told her that no one could go in without an admission fee. At that, my mother handed both her ticket and mine to the old man and to the young mother with the infant in her arms. They were allowed inside. But when my mother tried to push her way through after them, the two guards pushed her back with considerable force.

I can still see her, standing on a rock, frenziedly speaking to the crowd outside, telling them that those who cannot afford a bath have to wash themselves in filthy urine, while only a few meters away, the rich could bathe inside where there was plenty of the cleanest, healthiest water on earth.

"It is a criminal offense," she yelled, "for you to soak your sores in foul water. Follow me, and we'll show these mercenaries what we can do."

She barged past the guards right into the sulphur baths, followed by a small crowd of people who flung themselves into the warm, healing waters, while the guards took off.

Within an hour, while the sick and old were splashing about the baths, an army truck loaded with half a dozen soldiers pulled up at the doors. A command car followed the truck.

My mother was directing the movements of the bathers in her efficient, self-assured manner when the army officer, imposing in his smart uniform and ribbons, whip in hand, confronted her with a stern expression on his face. I felt nervous, wondering what he could do to her, but I saw her face him down when he asked if she, by any chance, was the troublemaker.

Slapping the whip across his thigh, he said, "You, Madame, have no right to take the law into your own hands, and you will be charged as a public nuisance, unless you tell these people to leave at once."

Instead of heeding the officer's advice, my mother turned to the crowd and told them to stay where they were. She seemed seized by some inexplicable frenzy. "This is God's water," she said, "it runs free, and these men in uniform have no human right to deprive you of it. Would they forbid the rain from falling from heaven?" she shouted in utter outrage.

The officer asked my mother to accompany him to his car. I stood by, watching the confusion around me. I could not hear their conversation, but, within a few minutes, the officer returned to the baths to announce that, from that day on, the spa was open to all, without any admission charge.

I could hardly believe my ears. I could not imagine what my mother could possibly have said to convince someone so sure and so angry, of such a change. But imagine the joy of those who heard the welcome news.

Chapter 26

My Mother, My Hero

I began to think that my mother must be some kind of saint, and I was aware that she did wield a certain amount of influence in those days. She also lived in a style the social milieu found, at times, hard to tolerate. But tolerate they did.

For instance, she bought me a bicycle when I was old enough to use one, after having been trained by Herunt, her bouncer at the theatre, how to ride it properly. She'd put on shorts, as I did, and we both went out cycling together, touring the city, when she was not busy performing. In those days, few women dared show their bare legs off stage, let alone go out in public with shorts while cycling and without the company of an adult male.

My mother could also drive a car. In fact, I never saw a female at the wheel of a car during all those years I spent in that city. My mother was the only one, it seemed. She often took me, Nevart, Nevart's husband, and her drummer for long rides. It was great fun.

I firmly believe that my mother and Isadora Duncan would have got along famously. From time to time, we would hear people whistle as we cycled by, but this did not faze my mother in the least. Often, we would stop outside the city limits, not too far from the Franciscan convent. We would sit on a rock somewhere in the shade of a tree, if we could find one, and eat our breakfast together, looking at the city from a healthy distance. At that early hour, the world would appear to be asleep, and we seemed to be the early birds. The streets were washed the night before, the sun was barely up, and the air smelt sweet. Sometimes my mother and I would race each other or play hide-and-seek, laughing our heads off. At such times we were more like sisters. Those pleasant times stand out to me like special pictures in a vast inspiring art gallery. It felt as if we owned the universe, although we both knew that the city, on the whole, could not have cared less about us.

Chapter 27

Snow

Growing up with my mother also included the magic of snow.

Days were fiercely hot with temperatures ranging from twenty-four to thirty degrees centigrade and even hotter at times. The trouble with these hot temperatures is that they lasted for many months. Winters, in contrast, were short.

It snowed every seven years or so, and then only for part of the night, just for a few hours. Everyone in the city would go wild, leaving their houses to run in the streets to welcome its whiteness; snow was like manna falling from heaven. Its sparkling magic—its ability to transform a hot dusty desert plateau, where water was a rare commodity due to a chronic shortage of rainfall, and where it was often rationed. Snow, indeed, was a memorable event.

When I saw the unexpected snowfall, I, too, would run out into the street in my housecoat with sudden exhilaration, followed by my mother and Marie, to find people already there rejoicing with childlike, uninhibited alacrity, celebrating the wonderful miraculous fall. We would clap hands and cheer and jump up and down trying to grab handfuls of the beautiful stuff, rubbing our sleep-filled faces in it. We'd also try to make snowballs out of it. I would try to save one tiny snowball, but by the time I ran back to my room, it would turn to water in the palm of my hand.

Chapter 28

A Pitiful Love Song

It was at about this time, I might have been eleven or twelve years old, that I began to develop a great fondness for movies. Sometimes, on weekends, I would go to the movies three times a day. Movies in the city were shown at three in the afternoon, then at six, and then at nine. If I wanted to see the same movie twice on the same day, I had to pay twice, unless the highly respected judge who was my mother's best friend and whom I called 'Uncle,' had given me his permission to use his loge.

If I had not been so busy seeing so many movies, especially those that featured Tino Rossi, the young Corsican singer who made females of all denominations swoon at his every syllable, maybe my scholastic life would have run more smoothly. I had a crush on him once I saw a movie called *Naples au baiser de feu.* I bought the soundtrack and the music sheets, and I learned most of his songs by heart. It was an obsession that was to change my life.

One day, my desk mate at the Franciscan school asked me to lend her the sheets with the lyrics from *Naples au baiser de feu* and some of the other, popular songs sung by Tino Rossi and other famous French singers we'd seen in recent movies. She wanted to copy out the lyrics. When she had finished copying some of them, she thanked me and placed them on my side of the desk. We thought no more of it until the following day, when the Mother Superior walked into the classroom, singled me out by name, and ordered me to follow her to her office.

As I followed the holy mother, silently walking over the marble floors I used to scrub, I idly wondered who had cleaned them that morning, and whether it was Josephine, for we used to share most of the chores when I was on the other side. I also wondered if my mother was ill or if something had happened to dear Marie, for her legs had been bothering her a great deal lately, but I was too scared to ask—besides, I was not given the chance to enquire.

The moment we arrived in the Mother Superior's office, she raised a fistful of music sheets in the air from behind her desk, with a painful expression of deep disappointment, her scolding voice shaking with rage, exploded in the small sanctum, sending fragments of phrases flying in my face. "Are these yours?" she asked.

"Yes, ma mère, they are mine. My mother bought them for me," I replied.

That response sealed my fate. During the long silence that ensued, I was puzzled by her state of shocked immobility. I was not sure of what to do, whether to walk back to my classroom, take the sheets of music from her, or stay and wait for her to say something.

She frowned, pressing her lips together tightly to form a straight mauve line. Ever since I had known the Mother Superior, ever since my orphanage days, I was convinced that if she ever bent forward, however slightly, she would topple over me like a marble colossus and crush me under her weight.

I took a small step back, as she sat at her desk and scribbled something on a sheet of paper, her waxen, wrinkled hand forming the words carefully. She then stood up with some effort, for she was a tall and thin woman, and handed me an envelope.

She must have read my mind about the music sheets, for she clung to them, adding that they contained all the evidence she required and that my mind was wallowing in filth. This was not at all suitable for my age, and I ought to be deeply ashamed to have such trash in my possession. I was then asked to go and pack everything I owned and to empty my classroom desk, for I would not be returning to the Franciscan School ever again. At that moment, I saw in my mind's eye the two nuns in the basement of the orphanage torturing the mouse with their hatpins—such a simple, easy gesture. A mere pin-prick. A few simple words in a letter, and that was that. Her word was law. The cage door was opened and I was released, expelled from the Franciscan convent with the blessings of the Mother Superior. Just as I had knelt on the rough recreation grounds of the orphanage to kiss the heavy iron cross in order to be absolved by her of the sin of disobedience, so now I was expelled for my unforgivable sin of owning copies of French love songs. She explained that she wished to see my mother that same afternoon, if possible.

My cheeks were flushed, and I tried hard not to cry. I was abashed beyond words. Another nun walked in. She was told to help me pack and accompany me to the exit and wait until our chauffeur arrived at noon to pick me up, as usual. The execution was final. The nun who had come to assist me was my piano teacher. I was fond of her. She accompanied me to the classroom I had come to love so much, and she watched me gather my belongings. My hands were shaking. I could not bring myself to look at my classmates, not even at my desk mate. She went on with her reading as though I was not even there. I wanted to say goodbye to her, but words failed me. I picked up my satchel and tiptoed out of the quiet classroom.

My piano teacher was *une mère*, as we called her. She walked me to the front of the convent school, where, only months earlier, Josephine and other orphans and myself had helped decorate the front entrance with dyed pebbles shaped like different flowers. I looked at the patterns for the last time, as if with new eyes. The memory was so strong that I looked down at my fingertips to see if there were any traces of the dyes still left there. The only traces left, however, seemed to be those of the orphanage; they had colored my views and my attitudes with a permanent stain.

As our car stopped outside, the nun took me by surprise. "I shall always pray for you, my child," she said, "no matter where you are in the world. I want you to remember this, always. I shall pray for you every night, no matter where I shall be. I shall pray for you until I die. You were my favorite piano student. Pursue your lessons. You possess great gifts. Take care. God bless you, my child. Adieu!"

I never expected to hear those words from a nun, and a superior nun for that matter. Even after so many decades, her words still ring in my ears. Her sad blue eyes reminded me of the kind nurse at the infirmary. Having barely finished her last sentence, the mother turned away, unable to face me without her mask of impassivity. The sound of her tiny footsteps disappeared around the corner. She did not turn back. Her white flowing robe was the last thing I saw of that saintly nun before she walked out of my life for good.

When I got home, my mother opened the letter. She read it once. Then she read it again as if uncomprehendingly. Then she began to pace the room with the letter still in her hand. She stopped to ask me whether she had it right. She wished to ascertain that the Mother Superior was talking about the popular songs that were on most people's lips in those days, about musicals, and the films that were being shown at the local theaters. I confirmed that it was true.

She looked shocked. She could not believe that the songs were filthy and that anyone who learned, sang, or listened to them possessed a filthy mind. She decided to go and see the Mother Superior right away. She got dressed and told me she would be back as soon as she could and that we might have dinner together. Since I was not allowed to return to that school, we had to make new plans regarding my education. She kissed me on the cheek and said, "Don't worry, darling, there are other schools. See you soon. Please don't fret too much. All right?"

I broke down and began to cry, but only because I loved school. I had been doing quite well. I had received a gold medal for my piano lessons. And I liked most of my teachers.

I waited I don't know for how long, but it seemed ages before my mother walked into the living room with a triumphant expression on her face. She was holding a large envelope. She asked me to sit down beside her on the settee after having told Marie to make her some Turkish coffee. Then, she opened the envelope and flattened the sheets of paper on her knees and said, "Look, sweetheart, these are some of the words that are responsible for your dismissal from the Franciscan School: 'Je voudrais t'offrir ma brune les trésors les plus beaux / Pour t'avoir au clair de lune / Un soir dans mon bateau.' Can you imagine anything worse?"

The English translation of these lyrics went something along the lines of "I would like to offer you my brunette the most beautiful treasures / To have you in the moonlight / One evening in my boat."

Then she laughed hysterically. And, turning her eyes up to the ceiling, she cried, "Oh why, oh why, what have we done to deserve this?"

She could not stop going over the lyrics of some of the songs, over and over again. Then, with an abrupt decisive gesture, she stood up and said, "Enough! No use breaking my heart over this. These so-called saintly women preach abstention, celibacy. If human beings listened to them, the world would become empty of humanity, of human beings. It is through love and procreation that they came to be. But they call this a sin. Love is one of the most precious feelings we are endowed with. Love.

Passion. Charity. When they sing their hymns, when they say, 'Jésus, Marie, Joseph, je vous donne mon coeur, mon esprit et ma vie,' are they not talking about love? Of giving? Jésus was a good man, we are told, and Joseph was Marie's carpenter husband—there is nothing wrong with those words. Celibacy is not a good or a bad thing. It is not for everyone, but those excluded ought not to be tainted as sinners. Love is a wonderful thing. Love of man, of woman, of mother and child, love is sufficient. It is prejudice that is a sin. Anyway, my love, I am rambling on. Enough! To hell with it! I will arrange for you to attend another school. I'll discuss it with some people I know. And they are in a position to help. Money will buy you education and I have enough of it, thank heavens, darling. Come. Worry not. Let's decide where to eat. It will give Marie the time off. She needs it. Look, sweetheart, before I give these sheets back to you, look at the lines they have underlined in red. Those are the sinful lines. What a sad thing this is. Really."

She handed me the bundle of sheets and gave me a huge, warm hug. "Go. Get ready. I'll have my coffee in the meantime." Turning to Marie, who looked concerned, my mother said, "Marie, we won't be eating dinner, or rather, my little girl will not be eating dinner alone, as usual. We are both going out to eat. Just to give you and Elias some rest. Tell Elias when he comes back from shopping. And you can go home after he leaves, if you wish, Marie, my dear."

"Then is your daughter not going back to the same school, Madame?" Marie asked.

"No, Marie, not to that same school."

For the next few days my mother kept reminding me to read about the Borgias, the family of Popes no less, and went on to add that there are things taking place in seminaries or boarding schools and orphanages and or convents far more insidious than the pitiful love songs of today.

Chapter 29

Uncle

I was soon registered as a boarder at one of the most expensive schools in the city, called The Immaculate Conception. And my expulsion from the Franciscan School in no way diminished my infatuation with Tino Rossi and other movie stars. I would walk by a particular movie theatre on Sunday afternoons to gawk at the picture of the brilliantined boy in the loose, long-sleeved, white satin blouse, à la Valentino, holding his guitar and smiling at me. My adoration of Tino Rossi grew with every film he made, until one day, when I could no longer contain it, I went straight to the manager's office and asked if he could spare one of Tino Rossi's photographs. He called me Chocolata. He smiled as he handed me a large, glossy picture of my hero.

I remembered how he had complained to the 'Honest Judge' because, in the past, I had invited too many friends to his loge at the movie theatre, because it was free. But I had stopped doing that for some time. Now, he looked pleased as he handed me the picture and said, "Please remember me to the judge."

Uncle stands out as a special person in my early life, though, as a child, I never expected his influence to become so pronounced. I am not sure when I began to call him "Uncle," but I think it was quite some time after my mother had made his acquaintance at the law courts regarding some minor legal matter when she walked into his chambers by mistake. He had then asked his clerk to help her out. He was most impressed by her beauty and invited her to have coffee with him.

He was not a big man. He might have been in his fifties. He wore glasses on his dark face, and his thick head of brush-cut hair was graying at the temples. He was spotlessly clean and always impeccably dressed in one of his two neatly patched suits, and he smelt of soap and after-shave lotion. His hands were brown and skinny, and his fingernails, cut short, were scrubbed several times a day. He ate little, rarely drank anything but water, and he never smoked. With his skeletal figure impeccably garbed in one of his gray suits, which he wore both winter and summer, he radiated a quiet dignity mingled with humble elegance. He wore gaiters over his well-polished shoes, and the only touch of color to his conservative attire was his bright tie and his red fez.

He walked and talked calmly as though measuring every word or action beforehand. I would say he possessed no special physical attributes, but he was no nonentity. He never shouted or lost his temper, yet he commanded respect and he could always make himself heard without ever raising his voice.

At first, he was by no means the precious friend he later became. He was just one of the male visitors who called on my mother from time to time, always at designated times in order to avoid unnecessary explanations, which would have proved to be rather awkward.

At times, I found myself taking part in these arrangements. After the servants had been let go for the day, I would be sent out to see a movie, and, as I left, I would padlock the door from the outside to make sure that people believed everyone was out. And when I returned after having seen the movie, I would look for a large safety pin on the window curtain inside the front door. If it were still there, it meant that I had to stay out a little longer and come back later. My mother and I worked perfectly as a team and we never got our signals crossed.

My mother often told me when we were alone that Uncle was the best friend she had ever had or would ever have. She trusted him and respected him. She told me that he was a Muslim, born in Turkey. She would shake her head and smile and say, "Here is an Armenian woman whose best friend is a Turk, my darling. Our best friend!" she would emphasize. She never showed any prejudice and she would say, "History is past, finished. Let politicians sort it out. We cannot carry grudges forever. People sign peace pacts, or armistices, and why not? New generations should look for peace and make a better world for themselves."

In fact, my mother taught Uncle the Armenian alphabet. He could read and write Armenian far better than I ever could. But what was different was that he used the Armenian alphabet to write letters in Turkish for my mother to read when she was on tour. Of course, he could not speak a word of Armenian. The analogy might be that of an English person, for example, using the Latin alphabet to form English words.

Even though Uncle had limited financial means, as the salary of a judge in those days in Syria was quite low, he was very generous. He lived in a modest district with his aged mother and unmarried sister who was a midwife. It was thanks to Uncle that I managed to see all those movies in a brief period of my adolescence and made a few fleeting acquaintances of my own age. But those girlfriends vanished into thin air as soon as the boxes at the movie house were closed to them.

Chapter 30

Powder Puffs

The sort of life I led made it difficult for me to form long-lasting friendships. My mother was often busy rehearsing, traveling, giving concerts, and going on tours, sometimes for long stretches at a time—leaving me in the care of servants in a large, empty house. Josephine, number 72, was my only real friend, and she was removed from my life when I left the orphanage. Convent life taught me a sense of emotional insularity that I have maintained to this day, perhaps to my loss.

One particular afternoon, I invited a handful of girls to our house while my mother was having some publicity pictures taken. We were having a great time, the five or six of us, playing with my mother's huge, soft powder puffs, some as large as our faces. We were blowing pink-, green-, and peach-colored powder all over her bedroom, while we kept jumping up and down on her bed in reckless abandon, as one might on a trampoline, giggling and screaming hysterically.

Much to our dismay, who should walk in on us suddenly but my mother. She scolded us and forbade the girls to ever return to our house. Since the orphanage would never have tolerated such goings-on, or such uninhibited hilarity, that was my first and last social encounter or adventure with people close to my own age and sex. I do not believe I ever laughed as heartily as I did on that crazy afternoon.

The only other brush with any sort of mutual friendship

occurred one time when my mother took me with her on tour to a nearby country. While she was performing in an Armenian operetta called *Ashug Gharib*, and the local pianist's daughter, Lili, and I began to spend time together. I cannot recall what we did, but we must have become good friends, for I remember the poignant scene the evening we said goodbye to her when I watched her walk away with her father, waving to us as the special bus was about to take us back home. I was not destined to form any long-lasting friendships for decades; my mother was my sole and constant companion.

Chapter 31

Immaculate Expulsion

On one of my mother's summer holidays, she told me that she would send me abroad to study law as soon as she had saved enough money. In the meantime, I went on with my schooling, doing my utmost to obtain the highest possible marks.

Unlike other schools I later attended in other parts of the world, the Immaculate Conception followed a different system in the classroom. When students were reciting or presenting their assignments, for instance, they were seated in order of academic achievement: the best students were seated at the front row, the second best next to them, and so on. The students at the back row were known to be the weakest students. Anyone entering the classroom could tell at a glance the academic standing of any particular student.

Sitting at the front row, being among the first students, I would often finish whatever recitation or presentation I had well before the rest of the class, so I got into the habit of scribbling down poems while only half listening to what was going on in the classroom.

One day, I was just putting the finishing touches to a series of verses, each line of which began with the words, "Je voudrais" ("I would like"), when, suddenly, the nun pulled the sheet of paper away from me. I was perhaps emulating Tino Rossi's "Je voudrais."

She read the poem, and then looked at me, her bespectacled eyes burning like two coals in hell, her cheeks twitching visibly.

"Did you write this – this?" In her outrage, she could scarcely find the words. When I told her that, yes, I had, she excused herself to the class and walked out with my poem in her trembling hand, leaving the classroom door wide open behind her.

No one dared move or utter a single sound. We all sat quietly as though cast in stone. I wasn't sure what was happening, but a sudden shiver ran through me and I was gripped by a sense of foreboding. I felt no sense of guilt. I wrote because I had nothing better to do. And I enjoyed writing poems and I still do. I really could not believe or accept the notion that my poem could have brought about the severe transformation in my teacher's demeanor. I wondered where she had taken my poem. I had finished my lessons, my turn had long passed because I was one of the top students in the classroom, and discipline had never been a problem…up until now.

Just as I was puzzling over these questions, she was back with another sister, still holding the same sheet of paper. She beckoned me to her. I rose and followed them, but not another word was spoken until we arrived at the Mother Superior's office.

The Immaculate Conception school had its main office on the ground floor. I remember hearing students playing in the small, square courtyard as we passed. I could not help recalling my incident with the Mother Superior at the Franciscan School. Until we entered the sacred room, I felt no feelings of guilt or embarrassment of any sort. Now, the same scene left me helpless.

The Mother Superior read my fourteen verses with open disapproval, her loathing mounting with every line. She was told that, I had, in fact, written them myself and during class. She affirmed that the two other nuns had also read them. Turning to me, she said it was sad that my mind worked in such a way. "What would make a nice, young lady, like yourself, write such obscene drivel?" My face burned with confusion. I said I did not know.

I was told to wait outside. I watched the door shut behind me. I stood in the narrow hallway listening to the wild thumping of my heart.

The nun's voice startled me. Back in the office, I was handed a sealed envelope to be given to my mother. I stared at the nuns in utter bewilderment.

When my mother woke up to have breakfast in bed as usual, I handed her the letter. She took it from my hand, looking me in the eye for a second before opening it. Her expression froze. She read the letter slowly, her color changing visibly. She seemed to devour each line with her eyes. I could see that the sheet on which I had scribbled the lines was being carefully held while she opened a smaller envelope, also with her name on it. After she finished reading it, she shook her head and said, "Look, darling, they have enclosed your poem with the letter of expulsion. How sweet!" Then she smiled and asked, "You wrote these verses during class, I understand?" I nodded, ashamed of myself. I expected her to scold me. She surprised me when she said, "These lines remind me of Tino Rossi's, 'Je voudrais t'offrir ma brune, les trésors les plus beaux / Pour t'avoir au clair de lune / Un soir dans mon bateau.' But you say, 'Je voudrais vivre / Entre tes bras jours et nuit / Je voudrais suivre / Le silence qui nous fuit;' "and you add, 'Je voudrais aussi / Dans un petit bateau / Bercée de poésies / Voir la lune sur l'eau.' Not bad, sweetheart."

I was surprised at her fantastic memory. I would have had some difficulty quoting Tino Rossi's lines, but my mother did not. After all, she was a trained actress. There was no sign of anger in her voice. Not only that, she turned to Marie, who looked concerned, and said, "I always imagined my darling daughter to study law in Geneva and become a lawyer somewhere in Europe. Now I see that we have a budding poet in our midst. So be it, Marie, my dear. Don't look sad. The nuns have sealed our fate."

Marie brought the Turkish coffee, and my mother settled down in her favorite armchair by the window where she normally sat and read, the breeze gently playing with the tulle curtains, her auburn hair catching the sun.

"I have a rehearsal this afternoon, darling," she said, "You can come to the theatre with us, if you wish, and sit and watch us rehearse. Maybe we will inspire you with some of the excellent lines, because today we are rehearsing parts of *La Dame aux Camélias*, the famous novel written by Alexander Dumas *fils*. There is also an operatic version of the play called *La Traviata* by Guiseppi Verdi. This is the stage play, sweetheart. It is simply wonderful. You'll love it. And sometime this week we will register you to another school, one close enough for you to walk there and back, if you wish."

The outcome of all this was that I was registered at the Lycée Français, a nondenominational, or secular, school. School began to mean something less than precious to me. I viewed the prospective lessons with cautious apprehension, expecting to be expelled at the slightest faux pas. In sum, school ceased to be a source of hope and pleasure.

Chapter 32

The Lycée Français

The Lycée Français was not a boarding school. It was a bit odd at first to be moving among men and women who did not wear uniforms. It was even stranger to hear a joke or a mild swear word, to hear teachers and students laugh out loud, and to hear students being teased by their teachers. Everybody acted so naturally, it was as though school was an extension of our home. Even so, I was careful not to show any incriminating song lyrics, and, above all, I made sure that I never wrote any poems at school.

As I viewed school from this new perspective, the attitudes of both teachers and students astonished me. Now it was they who found me slightly prudish, excessively courteous and watchful, but they were congenial, nevertheless. I did not know how to react, how to socialize. A remark uttered in jest by one of the professors before class would amaze me as much as the students' reaction, although it was never discourteous. They never thought twice about laughing out loud during lessons, and the teacher would wait for the laughter to subside before going on with the lesson. I could hardly believe my eyes.

With time, however, I began to relax a little. I became accustomed to the new way this special school was run. For instance, I became used to the routine where most of the students walked home for lunch, for, I, too, could walk home if I so wished.

A strange new feeling of freedom pervaded the whole school. The professors wore whatever they liked, and so did the students. We learned modern songs and sang them, along with our teachers. When I dared mention Tino Rossi, Fernandel, or Charles Trenet, for example, no one raised an eyebrow.

The teachers were friendly. I was particularly taken with Madame Poncelet, a tall, thin, wiry person of quick mind and movement. Her face was long and narrow and her expression, most pleasant. Her brown eyes were large and placid in spite of her somewhat sharp manner.

At the convent, especially at the orphanage, I was not permitted to stare or even look at a nun in the face. We had to lower our gaze to the ground in reverence of the holy figure in immaculate habits. But with Madame Poncelet, I felt at peace when I looked at her. I did not feel nervous or afraid, I did not feel humbled by her presence; on the contrary, I seemed to draw self-assurance, peace, and love from her calm and cheerful presence.

Madame Poncelet did not appear to mind my looking at her. She did not cringe. She would return my gaze and ask if I wanted some extra homework. She was always ready with the name of some excellent poet I should be acquainted with, and, as if by happenstance, she would produce a slim volume by Sully Prudhomme, Victor Hugo, Lamartine, Alfred de Vigny, or others. I would take the particular book of poems home and, after finishing my homework, I would curl up in my chair, alone in my bedroom, as if waiting for a special dessert after a good meal, and savor each word, or phrase, repeating those lines I could not let go. I never stopped marveling at the magic of words. That the mere juxtaposition of a series of letters should possess the power to reduce one to tears and another to hysterical laughter and that love, hate, passion, or ignorance could be expressed by so many alphabetical arrangements and play havoc with our feelings.

It was perhaps more than magic; it was a revelation, a miracle.

The pages in front of me would leap out, change form, wear costumes, and sing and dance. The very act of reading was a parade of jingles and music. Sentences were transformed into streets and colors, sunlight and flowers. I could almost smell the flowers hidden in the very letters and blink in their light. I could touch, with my heart and soul and eyes, eyelashes, and cheeks, and feel the coolness of the breeze, and smell the sea in the three letters that spelled it out.

Often, my mother would walk into my bedroom having just returned from the theatre, as late as two o'clock in the morning or even later at times, and she would gently reprimand me for staying up so late. I would then close the book reverently and place it under my pillow, so that the words in the book would now rest under my head, like a treasure chest with its jewels set in long lines. I would then sleep contentedly, relishing the thought that an almost duplicate copy of some of the poetic lines in the pages of the book under my pillow, rested above it, inside my head.

Another wonderful teacher was Madame Gotier. Among the many songs she taught us, one special one, about a beautiful rose, stands out. It was called, "Là-bas, là-bas, dans la prairie." The translated lyrics are as follows:

Over there, over there, in the meadow,
Over there, over there, in the meadow,
Keeping her white sheep, Belle Rose, Keep-
ing her white sheep

Chorus:
Beautiful Rose *of spring, Yes, of spring*
I met a Gendeville:
"How much do you earn per year?, Belle
Rose, How much do you earn per year?"

Ah! I don't earn much,
Ah! I don't earn much,
I only earn a hundred francs, Belle Rose,
I only earn a hundred francs
If you wanted to come to the city,
You would give twice as much, Belle Rose,
You would give twice as much,
I'm not going to the big city,
I'm not going to the big city,
Because my mother defends him, Belle Rose,
Because my mother defends him,
Over there, over there, I am loved,
Over there, over there, I am loved,
By a boy whom I love so much, Belle Rose,
By a boy whom I love so much,
And our love is for life,
And our love is for life,
Much more than your money, Belle Rose,
Much more than your money.

Many years later, I resurrected this song when I taught it to my own students. Madame Gotier made me realize that when knowledge is poured, so to speak, into another person's head, one's knowledge is not diminished; on the contrary, both teacher and learner are enriched by it.

My mother could not help but notice my renewed enthusiasm for school. One night, she sat on my bed in her elaborate stage dress and kissed me goodnight. "I see," she said, "that we did the right thing by enrolling you at the Lycée, my love. But you need to sleep. I am not scolding you, darling, but temper your enthusiasm with some logic, that's all. There is always tomorrow. Thank heavens you have finally fallen among real teachers and not preachers. A school ought to be the holy temple, or fount, of knowledge; not the source of distribution of fear and damnation."

I enjoyed every course, except that I could not grasp the rudiments of simple arithmetic. Other than that, I seem to have acquired knowledge with an obsession akin to greed. For instance, when a turbaned elderly gentleman came into our classroom for one period a day, every day of the week, to teach us Arabic, I learned that language with great enthusiasm and pleasure; what he taught us still remains with me today.

In spite of all the literature, and my mother's love of the theatre and of great masterpieces, I was living at a somewhat superficial level. In a sense, I was absorbing only a small percentage of what was really going on around me.

Chapter 33

Your Father Walked By

By the winter of 1940, as I was finishing elementary school, I was ready to obtain what was called the Certificat d'Etudes. The names of the graduates were read in alphabetical order before a massive crowd of students and anxious parents. My mother was at rehearsal that day, so she could not attend the event. We were gathered in the open air not too far from a river that was overflowing its banks at the time.

Madame Poncelet was standing beside me while I waited to hear my name to be called, watching the floodwaters in the distance. Finally, all the surnames that started with A ended, and my name had not been called. I was so disappointed that I gave one quick glance at the river and seriously considered running and throwing myself in it, but Madame Poncelet took me by the arm and told me to wait. I had not realized until then that I had been registered under H, under my father's assumed surname, and not under my mother's name.

True enough, my name was called out and we walked together towards Monsieur Martel to receive my first graduation diploma. I had a total of about four and a half years of education, maximum, not counting the years at the orphanage: almost a year at the Franciscan school, under a year-and-a-half at the Immaculate Conception, and two wonderful years at the Lycée Français.

I was sad to be leaving the school and upset that I was not going to see Madame Poncelet again. When I told my mother what had happened on graduation day, she explained that it did not really matter whose last name I was given, that it was not worth changing it. Then she told me that my father had passed by our house one afternoon that previous summer. Even though we were both sitting side-by-side on the balcony, eating fresh pistachios and looking out on to the street, she did not bother to point him out to me. She did not want me to see him, she told me. He was out of prison because the new President had pardoned all prisoners, but she had heard that my father was leaving for Erevan, in Armenia, as were many other Armenians.

I have never forgotten that. There was the man whose name I bore, whose child I was, yet my mother was capable of letting him pass by our house without saying a word to me about him.

It was not till years later that my mother explained to me why she let him pass that day. She told me that she met my father, for the first time, from across a room, at an arranged family dinner. She was fourteen years old, and she hated him on sight. The next time they met, they were in church exchanging vows. Up to that point, they had barely said two sentences to each other. My mother told me that my father was a good poet. Apparently, he came from a good family.

Soon after my parents were married, he was unfaithful. When she confronted him about it, he attacked her with a knife. Luckily, she survived, but he tried to kill her a second time after I was born. This time, he used an axe. Her relationship with her parents and her brother became strained because they expected her to tolerate my father's behavior. She decided to run away with me from Turkey to Syria, escaping from him—and her family—for good.

Chapter 34

World War II

Not long after my graduation from the Lycée Français, Madame Poncelet and all the school staff left for France. The Lycée was shut down. We were in the thick of the Second World War and also of another local uprising against the French.

My mother was concerned about sending me abroad to continue my studies because she had read in the papers and heard on the radio that a man named Adolf Hitler—a name we had never heard before—was trying to invade certain countries in Europe and that his plan was to master the whole of Europe, if not the world. She wondered how or where I was to pursue my studies when, all of a sudden, the world appeared to have become politically, socially, and economically unstable.

As the Second World War progressed, we began to take a serious interest in the events. Martial law was declared, and there was a general strike. In 1939, the French had taken the drastic step of suspending the Syrian constitution and put the Ministries of Defense and Foreign Affairs under their control. They wanted to hold tightly onto their colonies or countries under their mandate. They had invested heavily in education. They ran the Institut des Lettres Orientales at the University of St. Joseph in Beirut, apart from the expensive convent schools and lycées, which were segregated as either boys' or girls' schools.

The ill feeling of the local population for the French went back to the 1920 San Remo Conference that gave the French the right to control Syria. French forces had invaded Syria, overthrowing the Arab government in July of the same year. Syria was partitioned in 1920 under the terms of the mandate. A mandate, however, is neither a protectorate nor a colony. It is supposed to be transitory, yet the French had stayed in Syria, in spite of the numerous uprisings, for a period of about thirty years. The local population felt that the French were led not by goodwill, but by rather excessive self-interest.

At the crux of the matter was Article 4 of the League Mandate, which was contravened by the League of Nations because they gave away any territory that was held in trust without the slightest struggle. Lebanon, for instance, which was part and parcel of Syria at one time, was created as a new state that same year and that distressed the Arabs. Christian minorities seemed to be favored by the French. Syria was run from the Quai d'Orsay in France and not by the majority Arab population in Syria.

The partition of Syria into what the French termed "the Levant States" and the giving away of an important Mediterranean port (Alexandretta, or Sanjak) to the Turks in 1938 gravely upset the Arab majority. The Arabs, therefore, seized the occasion of the defeat of France by the Germans during the Second World War, to oust the French from Syria once and for all. The Arabs rose in revolt, but the French met force with force and arrested all the Arab leaders.

While my mother and I were reasonably safe at home, we could not avoid witnessing some of the local rage that manifested itself in the streets of the city, in shootings, in marches, in outcries, in threats, and in strikes. There were times my mother could not work or travel, and we sometimes found ourselves short of coffee or sugar or even bread for a few days, but Elias was a genius at replacing the staples before we suffered too seriously.

Our house became a veritable Tower of Babel of diverse political opinions. My mother's lawyer friend, who called on her regularly at ten o'clock in the morning when she was available, pestered her with his belief in the superiority of the British and the Americans. I would often sit and listen to them.

Most North African soldiers in the French army or the Legionnaires were held in healthy respect by the local civilian population, for they were considered to be fierce fighters. We never witnessed any atrocities. But others did. My mom's friend Nevart—the woman who witnessed my mother smashing her fine china—lost her only son, Nerkess, who was about my age, when he was hit by a stray bullet while running home from school one day having been caught in a cross fire.

Of course, many innocent people were being killed in these skirmishes, and I was often scared, but my mother would take me in her arms, comforting me as best as she could. It was not war, as such, but, perhaps, a civil war, without proper leadership, for soon, the shops would re-open, the grocers would return to their raffia chairs sipping their drinks, smoking their narghiles, and playing tric-trac as if nothing had happened.

Chapter 35

Home Becomes A Stage

My mother took little or no serious interest in local politics until the war was almost over, even though she admitted to me that she would argue with some of her male visitors just to entertain them. She was born in Turkey, she spoke Turkish, she was an Armenian Orthodox, and she attended church every Sunday. She believed that all men were equal, and all we could do was to keep out of harm's way without hurting anyone else. She always said, "Trust people, but watch them at the same time." She had an aphorism for every occasion.

"No human being is better than the other. We are all governed by an incomprehensible force, a destiny, that deals our cards, and we cannot help being born in a certain country; we cannot choose the color of our eyes, or skin, or religion, or control our future. We are born naked and we go naked, darling."

My mother attempted to inculcate in me a sense of distrust, a sense of caution in dealing with most people. She was cunning beyond belief. She always reiterated and cautioned me against the complexities of a man's heart and the contradictions that lay therein.

At the same time, she would, at the drop of a hat, help anyone by offering her own bed. She even seemed naive at times, but, as I was still young, I had no basis for comparison.

Alongside the occasional political argument, my mother would entertain her guests with music. She played the lute to perfection, as well as the piano and the mandolin, as had my grandfather.

I had now become emotionally insular in a house full of boisterous, friendly men. I found nothing in common with them, for I was a teenage girl growing up among the professionals around me. I would sit and listen to their conversations less and less often. It was interesting to watch them come and go, but I felt as though our house had become a stage of some sort, and I was a lone member of the audience. I enjoyed it most when I was alone with my mother, but those times were rare.

Chapter 36

Men Are Pigs

In spite of her busy life, my mother watched over me, surveying every little glance or movement on the part of her numerous male guests. The slightest doubt in her mind would trigger a sudden rage, so much so that she would decide never to see that particular person again, no matter how wealthy or influential he was.

She once threatened me by taking me up to our rooftop, which, like many Mid-Eastern rooftops, was flat and unprotected, without a surrounding wall for safety.

Holding me dangerously close to the edge, she pointed down to the street below and said with harsh intensity, "If you allow anyone, darling, to kiss you, or to touch you before you are married, I will push you off this roof. Do you understand?"

She then embraced me and cried a little, explaining that she herself was finished, that she was living only for me, to see me make my way in life, to see me obtain what she called my invisible "Golden Bracelet of Independence."

I was not to rely on any man, for men were pigs, she would remind me. There are a few good ones among them, she admitted, but not too many. She felt that Uncle was, perhaps, among the few good ones, but she was not too sure of that yet, for he was embarrassed to be seen with her in public, and he visited her secretly, even though he was a single man. And he would never dare ask her to marry him. She believed all this.

She believed, most of all, in education. I knew that my independence meant the world to my mother. She devoutly wished to see me practice law, and, yes, I could still write poems if I so desired. "Besides," she added, "some of the greatest doctors, painters, and lawyers have written great poems and great books. I can name two off-hand, Chekhov and Somerset Maugham."

My mother then told me the story of a Greek philosopher who, upon the destruction of a city, refused to pack up his belongings and the king enquired why he was leaving all his treasures behind. The philosopher replied that he was not, and pointed to his head. "All the wealth in the world," my mother added pointing to her head, "resides in the sublime box called the brain, sweetheart. I forget the philosopher's name. I am too excited for some reason. Anyway, all is in the sublime box here."

Chapter 37

Growing Up Fast

When summer came again, I borrowed a motorcycle and started going for rides. One day, I asked Anush to come with me, but I accelerated instead of slowing down when we were turning a corner, and we both went flying into the ditch. I ended up with a stone in my right leg, just below the knee, two smashed elbows, and other minor injuries. Incredibly, Anush got up, shook the dust off her skirt and came to my rescue. My leg healed quickly. I was not affected so much by the accident (except for the scar on my leg), but by my mother's anger when she learned of the accident. That was my last motorcycle ride.

Perhaps because she rode, my mother did not seem to mind my learning how to ride horses. A friend of hers, Louis, who owned stables and many horses, let me ride any time I wanted. I was growing up fast and learning something each day, it seemed.

While my mother was on tour, I started taking up boxing. Herunt brought me a twenty-five kilo bag of sand, and he hung it from my bedroom ceiling so that I could practice my punches. He would drop in once in a while to see how I was progressing.

At a time when gender roles were pretty clear, maybe I was unconsciously absorbing the qualities of the men around me by slowly attempting to become a boy. Or maybe it was that time of life when I knew little about my own body and I was a little confused. Biology was never taught at schools, so I knew nothing or very little about the female anatomy. We had studied some chemistry, but nothing was taught about the human body.

Whatever it was that motivated me into frantic physical activity, I began to develop strong arms and legs. My summer routine differed from the winter one, in that, in the summer, on most days, I woke up much earlier, just before dawn, put on my shorts and went cycling alone. I would grab the bike my mother had bought me and I would go struggling uphill and flying downhill in a maniacal manner. My body seemed to fly along the empty streets under the rising sun while birds chirped and trees sighed before being trapped under the merciless sun. The sun rose and set quickly in that part of the world. It was either day or suddenly, night. The long, awe-inspiring, wide-open skies, the magnificent low Canadian sunsets lay far ahead in the future.

It was after my mother's return from a three-month tour that she noticed something was wrong with my posture. She was sitting, having her coffee as usual, when she put her cup down and stood beside me. She took me by the hand and asked why I was all hunched up.

"What's the bump in the middle of your back, darling?"

As she held me by the shoulders in an attempt to straighten me up, she found a great big knot at the center of my back, under my blouse. My posture typically required some correcting, in spite of the nuns' method of pricking our backs with hatpins, but I could not hide the slump caused by tying a scarf under my blouse, right across my chest. The knot gave me away.

At her questioning, tears filled my eyes. I felt ashamed. I blurted out that my chest was swelling. I told her I thought it was because of the boxing. Boxing must have expanded my chest area, I said.

Gently, she undid the knot and pulled away the silk scarf she had bought me when she had come back from one of her tours.

"What boxing lessons are you talking about, darling?" she asked, confused.

I explained that I had been practicing every day during her absence, and that Herunt had hung the punching bag in my bedroom. I took her to the bedroom to see it, and there she asked me to sit on my bed beside her, and for the first time, she seemed to find it hard to speak.

After a long pause, she sighed and took me in her arms.

"My darling, you are becoming a woman. This is a beautiful phase of life," she told me. She went on to explain the intricacies, reassuring me that it was all perfectly natural to have one's chest swell, adding with a charming smile, "All young ladies' chests swell, sweetheart. It is normal. Don't cry, please darling. It happened to me when I was about your age." Then, she kissed me on the cheek. Hers was wet, too.

All those months I had been torturing myself, wondering why those two distinct protrusions had appeared on my chest, never connecting the fact to a natural process. We remained seated on that pink satin bedcover in my bedroom for a long time before my mother decided to call Marie to take the wretched sand bag down. Despite being very advanced in her thinking about women, some of my mother's ideas about women's roles were not progressive.

She smoothed my hair back with her hand, calming my heart and my nerves. She told me that she was most upset by the fact that I had been growing up during her absence. "Where have I been all this time, darling?" she asked, weeping. "What kind of a mother am I?"

The following day, she subjected Herunt to a barrage of questions about my boxing lessons.

"Who's paying you??" I heard her shout. "It is not your place to make these decisions! Not to mention you've ruined the ceiling in Anahid's room!"

Herunt sat, stone-like, taking all this abuse into his great big hulk. I believe he was the largest man I ever saw. He had been a pugilist and had a cauliflower ear that affected his hearing somewhat. It fascinated me. But that day, my mother more than compensated for Herunt's hearing loss by shouting loud enough for the whole neighborhood to hear. I doubt whether Herunt missed a single syllable of her utterances.

I had often observed my mother's fearlessness and the power she exercised over most people around us. It was remarkable that she could dominate such a Hercules of a man, and, yet, he could have got up and squeezed the life out of any one of us with one huge hand. Instead, he apologized, promising never to decide anything without first consulting her, and then he went and took his jacket and disappeared from sight.

Chapter 38

Haig Meets Herunt

One summer day, I saw a man, about thirty years old, lying flat on his back on the sidewalk, frothing at the mouth, his eyes upturned, his body seized in a spasm. I skirted the sidewalk in order to avoid any contact, as I was quite startled by the bizarre scene. But other people soon came to his rescue. The young proprietor of a nearby store came out and placed a pencil between the epileptic's teeth.

The whole scene took about half an hour. I stood back watching. Then the body seemed to come back to life. The man stood up, shook the dust off his suit, while his new friend slapped his face gently, several times, then led him into a tailor's shop nearby, sat him down, and gave him some coffee.

I had almost forgotten the incident when, a few days later, I happened to be passing by the same tailor's shop, where I recognized the young man who had offered his pencil. He greeted me and said that he ought to reassure me about the man's state of health, explaining that these fits could occur at any time, and at any place, that it was fortunate in a sense that the victim had fallen on the sidewalk and not in the middle of busy traffic. I nodded. He asked me if I wanted some lemonade. Remembering my mother's advice about talking to strangers or taking anything from them, I declined.

The next time I passed by the same shop, the same young man appeared to be waiting for me, his huge blue eyes bright with welcome. I learned that his name was Haig.

"Hello, again!" he said, in Armenian. He was thin and reasonably tall, with gentle manners and kind eyes. I found the stranger handsome, courteous, and attractive. He had a fair complexion and he spoke Armenian.

"Come, have a lemonade. It's hot out today. It won't hurt!"

He saw me hesitate. He smiled and asked, "Tell me who you are."

I thought that everyone knew who we were because my mother's pictures were seen on placards in most parts of the city. I told him who I was, with a touch of pride.

"Really? Then you must come in. Please!"

I considered the invitation with deliberate caution. What harm would there be in a chat on a sunny day in an open store with such a courteous and hospitable young man, I asked myself. Then I followed him in, had a large glass of lemonade, and bragged a little about my mother's popularity. He seemed to consider me attentively. Then, some clients walked in. I finished my drink, thanked him, and went on my way feeling quite pleased.

Now I expected a glass of lemonade each time I happened to be going by that store. With time, Haig found out all about me and about my mother, such as our routine, her tours, and more.

One evening, a few weeks later, I heard a knock on our front door. Marie had gone home. Maurice had driven my mother to the theatre, and they were not due back until about two o'clock in the morning. And Elias was out, too. The house was empty except for me.

A shiver ran through me. It was Haig. Why would he call on us, I wondered. He must have known that my mother was not at home to greet him, and, besides, I had not mentioned him to anyone. What was I to do? Open the door, or speak to him through the window to tell him to come back when my mother was home?

I opened the window in the door and spoke to him through the bars. I told him that it was late, that my mother was at the theatre and would not be back until the early hours of the morning. I said that I was sorry and that I could not ask anyone in because I was alone in the house.

"At seven o'clock in the evening," he teased. "Can't we just sit and chat like two civilized human beings, at least for half an hour? I came all this way to see you," he added. Then, "My car is parked outside your house—perhaps you would like to go and see a movie with me? We would be back well before your mother returns from the theatre," he added.

I hesitated for a moment, but then said, "No, I cannot see you. My mother does not know anything about you."

"Well, then," he said, smiling, "you can introduce us to each other. I hear that she is a very liberal and civilized lady."

Something in me wanted to trust the stranger who had offered me so many glasses of lemonade.

Finally, I opened the door and in he walked. I made him some orangeade, and we sat facing each other. I kept thinking how pleasant and courteous he was. We must have chatted for about half an hour when I heard a key in the lock of the front door, and in came my mother with Herunt.

I recall the tall glass of orangeade, now empty, resting by the little table beside Haig as we sat across from each other. I remember telling him about the marvelous pictures of movie stars that my mother had once brought me after one of her long tours, when we were brutally interrupted. It must have been my mother's intention to create such a scene so that I would remember it for as long as I lived.

Herunt lunged forward, grabbed the helpless Haig by the lapels, lifted him high off the ground, and brought him back down again, crushing his legs under him as Haig buckled under and fell to the floor. A spurt of blood jerked out of his mouth as Herunt slapped his delicate face. He then picked Haig up again with his right hand and punched him again with his left.

All this time, my mother uttered not a single word. Herunt was given a free hand, and he was in his element. I was hiding in one of the farthest corners expecting the same treatment any minute. Finally, my mother spoke. "Enough! The bastard has learned his lesson. Take him away and drive him home. And remember, Herunt, not a word to anyone."

When Haig was carried out to his car and the front door was shut, my mother turned to me. I felt sick. My heart went out to Haig but I dared not utter a single sound. I expected to get flogged or starved to death or sent back to the orphanage, for my mother had used that threat on more than once occasion in the past for my minor transgressions.

Her first question to me was, "Did the bastard touch you?" Then, without waiting for an answer, added, "I know he didn't because we have been following his movements for weeks, ever since he first spoke to you outside his store."

I was astounded. Until that moment, I did not know that my mother was having me followed. My limbs felt loose and my tongue was paralyzed. Cold tears fell slowly, one by one, like drops of ice. I could only stare at her calm face.

She wanted to know why I had entered the stranger's shop, and what did he want from me, exactly.

I shook my head incredulously. Surely this was a nightmare. I wondered whether Haig would live, whether his legs were broken, whether he would ever walk again. And what would he think of my mother now, after I had so highly praised her to him? What would he think of me? I took in my mother's whole face with disbelieving eyes. My knees were so weak I wanted to sit down, but I was too terrified to move.

She said that Haig will have learned his lesson and would never dare attempt anything so foolish again in his life, adding a few familiar homilies—that this was a brutal world, a man's world, and to survive we had to be even more brutal than they. Then she opened her arms wide and I fell into them, shivering from head to foot.

In a world where most women were defenseless, I later learned to appreciate my mother's terror at seeing a stranger call on me during her absence. She repeated often that she had to act at once, for later would have been too late.

Much later, when we spoke about that awful scene with Herunt beating Haig, my mother told me a tale, a parable, if you like, about a man named Hodja whose son was about to bring back some water in an earthenware jug from a communal well.

Before he left, Hodja turned to the boy and slapped him across the face, saying, "Be careful now, son, don't go and break the jug. It's the only one we have."

"But, father," responded the startled boy, "I have not even left yet, and the jug is not broken."

"What would be the use of slapping your face after you break the jug, my son?" the father asked.

It was bad enough for a girl to be seen in broad daylight with a young man to whom she was not engaged, let alone for her to receive a male visitor into her home during her mother's absence and after dark. The loss of a girl's virginity was considered worse than a crime. It was a disgrace, a dishonor, a calamity, an indelible stigma for life. No judge or jury, nor priest or sheikh could absolve such a mortal sin.

It was therefore this precious gift, this fragile reputation that my mother was fighting to save. She employed a man's muscles to safeguard my chastity, which was of uppermost importance, at least, in the part of the world we lived in. The best way for her to defend me was to have the stranger's face slapped, so to speak, before the jug was shattered.

Chapter 39

Golden Bracelet Of Independence

My mother trusted no man. She did not believe that a man could love a woman for what she was—for her kindness, generosity or her honesty, or even her talent. As far as she was concerned, a man was there to use a woman as a sex object; she was, as she described it, a hole in the mattress.

She also dreaded the word "love," when it involved a male. To her, the only true love was maternal or filial love, or love of humanity in the abstract, which included men and women, and that had nothing to do whatsoever with the relationship between individuals.

The best my mother could offer a man, therefore, was the semblance of tenderness or fondness. Yet, she was never coquettish; she was far too subtle for that. And she never fell in love, never felt a lasting affection or a sense of deep loyalty towards any man.

My mother was fortunate to have the unquestioning love of such a fine human being as Uncle's. He began as a lawyer and was now a Supreme Court judge. This dark, diminutive man with the coal-fierce bespectacled eyes was endowed with a self-effacing humility that bordered on sainthood. He was congenial but always withdrawn, with a remarkable acceptance of man's general plight on earth. A born fatalist, like Job, he thanked Allah for everything. Though a judge most of his life, he could boast of no worldly possessions worth mentioning. He did not own a car.

In all the years I was privileged to know Uncle, I never heard him utter an uncivil word, display anger or resentment, or speak ill of anyone. He sometimes helped me with my math lessons whenever he could, and once a week, on Friday, he would leave me five pounds on my school satchel.

On most days, he would arrive after lunch, spend a short while with my mother and then return later in the evening, after supper.

When he came in the afternoon, he would walk over to the hat-stand by the front door, hang up his fez, then sit down on the living room settee beside my mother, always in the same seat, always beside her, facing me. But he never sat too close to my mother.

Although he greeted us with genuine warmth, it was done with a sort of serenity, an indefinable and beautiful calm. I could tell from his facial expression that he felt delighted to be with my mother. He looked like a little boy who had won some sort of prize.

With touching courtesy, he preferred me not to know the extent of their relationship, so for that reason, he came back after I had gone to bed. He spent most of the night in my mother's bedroom and left our house at dawn, just before Marie or Elias were due to arrive. He never allowed my mother to touch his hand or to kiss him. If she occasionally displayed the slightest exuberance, he responded with the greatest restraint. I can still hear him whispering to her with some slight embarrassment, "Please, not in front of your child."

At times, he appeared perturbed because of the burden of office. If he accepted a cup of Turkish coffee, which was rare, he would sip it slowly while relating some troubling incident. One afternoon, he told us that he had just sentenced a man to death, sealing his fate forever. "I shudder," he said, "when I consider whether all the evidence in the world against any culprit justifies the penalty of death. Victor Hugo wrote about it. You know, in *Le Coupable,* I believe, to show the futility of such a trial. An innocent man was tried and sent to his death when the real criminal was found sometime afterwards."

On a few occasions, Maurice drove us to the law courts where we waited, anxious and proud, to be admitted into Uncle's chambers. Once outside, he would ask his male secretary to serve us drinks, and I'd often walk away with a pocketful of assorted candies he kept in his desk drawer.

My mother's beautiful hazel eyes would shine with a new glow when she spoke about Uncle. "We have a good man here, darling," she would say, as if assessing a thoroughbred horse. And then, "We must play our cards right; otherwise we'll lose him." Then she would add her underlying distrust of men, "Why, he could even have me deported back to Turkey if he wanted to. Mind you, he's not a cruel man, but you never know with men—they can't be trusted, sweetheart." And yet, Uncle, too, was born in Turkey.

One day, feeling a little bolder, I asked her if she felt any love for Uncle. She was sitting by the window, looking like a queen, the morning light reflecting the warm glow of her hazel hair, still uncombed, her beautiful peacock housecoat spread on the settee like a colorful fan on each side. She had had her canine tooth removed, a perfectly good tooth, to have it replaced by a gold one and with a tiny diamond encrusted in it. Every time she smiled, the diamond shone in the light. She enjoyed joking about it by saying, in Turkish, that she had a truly bright smile. I believe it was in fashion at the time, but I don't remember ever seeing anyone else with a diamond-encrusted gold canine tooth.

She considered my question for a while and said, "I like him more than any other man in the world, sweetheart. But I must be careful all the same. He is powerful." She ruffled my hair and sighed, as the sparkle in her eyes faded somewhat. When

I asked her whether she would ever marry Uncle, she laughed and told me to go and get myself ready to be registered at the American Missionary College for Girls.

When we were about to leave, she stopped for a second to say, "Darling, don't ask me if I would ever marry Uncle. Ask whether Uncle would ever consider marrying me. Come. Let's go. Maurice is waiting."

My mother wanted me to learn English which, according to her, was going to be the most important language in the world. "The best way to sell English to the poorer population in a country where education costs the earth," she mused, "was to make learning it as cheap as possible. It is a wonderful thing to do. I believe that education should be free. Anyway, it is used as the American carrot dangling before the less well-off population, among which are many Armenians. It is another way of saying that knowledge is power, and education is going to be your invisible Golden Bracelet of Independence in this crazy world. My weapon is my appearance and my singing talent. Yours will be your education."

She herself had studied English in Adana, Turkey, where she was born, sometime around the First World War. And that was when General Allenby had visited my grandfather's home and had tea with the family. She was proud of that. General Allenby fought in Syria against the Turks and took Aleppo, the biggest city, and also Damascus, the capital. The visit of such a dignitary would indicate a respect with which my grandfather was held.

I vaguely recollect my grandfather's long narrow face, decorated with a handlebar mustache, and his dark eyes. He appeared impressively lanky to me as a mere child, but anything else I know of my grandfather comes to me second-hand from my mother. I gathered that my grandfather was a well-traveled gentleman with a deep fondness of music and literature. He had been to

Egypt, Mesopotamia, and Syria. In Hama, in central Syria, he had sat for days on end by the Orontes River, the Nahr-al-'Asi, in Arabic, at the foot of the noria, an undershot waterwheel of the bucket type used in primitive irrigations systems, to hear and record the delightful moans and groans of this great Roman waterwheel loaded with a chain of rusty pots as they rose and fell before him.

The influence of General Allenby's visit must have left a strong impression on my mother, because she began to read the newspapers in English, and she often quoted passages from them. One was that the Americans were trying to gain influence through the Protestant Missionary Center in Boston, Massachusetts, where they sold education in exchange for their religion. "Just like the French," she explained. She believed that Syria was in a desperate shape because advanced nations would not help it to become independent, and that they preferred to keep the people they controlled in a weak state, or uneducated, so that they couldn't use their knowledge to resist the onslaughts. "I recently read in the papers," she said, "which was funny, darling, that the missionaries in the city were handing out sacks of flour to some who became converted to their religion. What was amusing was the headline read, in Turkish: 'Un biti. Din biti.', meaning, 'Flour finish. Religion finish.' That apparently applied to those who reverted to their original religion after their sack of flour was used up. Anyway, we don't care. Marie's daughter attended that school, and I was glad to be of some help."

All the way in the car during our trip to the American College for Girls, my mother kept expanding on the subject. Now and then, I would throw a glance at Maurice's implacable face. I could not help thinking that he was, I felt, a cardboard character. He never laughed. He rarely spoke. He just drove us wherever my mother ordered him to. My mother was used to his expressionless face, so she kept on talking.

"It is all part of the power struggle," she said. "But I don't care what they do, provided you are safe, provided you get your education, and you become independent. We are all beggars, not choosers, my love, so we must remember that everything has its price, and we must make sure that we are not undersold, that's all."

Chapter 40

Skipping Grades & Invading Countries

The significance of my mother's words did not fully register until much later in my life, when I began to appreciate the subtleties of human barter at which she was skilled. Though she never once used the word, almost everything she said was colored by the way she set prostitution against religion, which she named as the root of most of this world's evils. "How could anyone, in the name of religion, kill another human being?" she often asked.

These themes, repeated ad nauseam, and with variations by my dear mother, sometimes brought in Jesus Christ, who was a great man because he forgave Mary Magdalen. She told me all about casting stones at a sinner, then added, "Aren't they still doing that? Don't some people cast stones at us because we love going to the movies and singing love songs, and riding bicycles wearing our shorts? How dare we show our bare legs in public and ride bicycles in broad daylight?"

Finally, we arrived at the American Missionary College for Girls, which was distinct from the American Missionary College for Boys, and which was situated further outside the city. The Girls' school took about an hour to get to from where we lived. Within a few days I started to attend the school that Anush had attended for years, thanks to my mother's help. I felt a bit odd doing that, but I said nothing about my feelings to my mother because I knew she would take me back to the famous Bon

Marché with her and have yet another picture taken by Ruba, in color and framed, to be hung in my bedroom, over my head, like the Sword of Damocles.

At the American Missionary School for Girls, or the American College for short, my frustration seemed to increase every hour of the long day because they spoke nothing but English. It was an immersion school, and I felt lost. Students asked me questions in English, but I could not answer them. I did not know what they were saying, although they all seemed friendly.

I well recall the first sentence our teacher wrote on the blackboard. It read, "Some people earn money." No one used a word in a different language to help me understand what it meant. Looking back, I believe that it was a wonderful system—it was the best way to learn a language. But at that time, I found the language strange and unpleasant sounding, especially when I had been used to speaking Parisian French.

Even when I got home and complained to my mother that I felt lost at school, she insisted that I persevere. She kept on harping on the importance of the English language and she said that Shakespeare had written the best of anything any author could write and that once I had become accustomed to the new sounds, she bet that I would fall in love with the language. She kept repeating over and over again, "Don't worry, you will soon latch on, darling! Study! Concentrate! Remember you got top marks in French at the Lycée—remember they called out your name and said, 'Tableau d'honneur, avec félicitations,' that's something to be proud of, and every report card you brought home said, 'Très bonne élève. Mauvaise en mathématique.' I don't care about the mathématique bit, you did well indeed. So keep going, sweetheart!"

So I tried to keep going. I studied and listened and learned, and in a short time, my head cleared as the language became more intelligible. I even skipped two classes in my first year. On top of that, I wrote poems in English. Both my mother and Uncle were proud of my progress at school. They had, in fact, taken it for granted. My English grammar was a bit weak at the start, but thanks to one of my mother's lawyer friends that, too, improved with time.

During this time, the war in Europe was still raging. Hitler marched through Europe with his mighty German army as one would though a park. One European city after another fell to the Germans. My mother, and sometimes Uncle if he was able to visit us that day, listened to the radio, and my mother read several different newspapers—the city was known for its proliferation of newspapers in different languages and from different viewpoints—trying to keep abreast of the latest news as much as possible.

One day, my mother asked Fred, another lawyer friend, whether she had made a mistake by sending me to an American school instead of having me learn German. She wondered whether she had been rather hasty in her decision to focus on English.

Her friend reassured her that the British were going to win the war and that she need never regret her decision—he concurred that English was going to be the most important language in the world. But my mother did worry. She argued with him that the British were unprepared, that they had no U-boats and no air force to speak of, that Hitler could land his army on British soil and encounter no resistance whatsoever, and that even the French were weakening under German pressure.

But with a wave of his manicured hand, he dismissed my mother's theories. He admitted, nevertheless, that Gabriel Puaux, the French high commissioner, was siding with the Vichy government and collaborating with the German commission in Syria because he wanted to be on the winning side, but all that would change soon, he smiled optimistically, while his thick bushy eyebrows almost fell over his big, bulging blue eyes. He was light complexioned, had a rather long face, with fat jowls, and straight light brown thinning hair that might have been blond when he was a boy. He was taller than the average citizen, somewhat on the podgy side even at his age, which was about thirty-five or thereabouts.

Unlike Uncle, he wore the best suits and ties and beautiful brogues and came from a wealthy family. He was as affluent as he was generous and successful at his law practice. And he seized every opportunity to tease my mother. He would roll his bulging eyes comically under the dark, threatening eyebrows and long lashes, and remind my mother that one of her dancing partners, a certain colonel, was fighting on the side of the Vichystes. If he knew about my mother's other friends, he did not seem to care. And my mother played along, always pretending to get upset. "I don't care on whose side he is, at least he gave the poor people a free sulfur bath, damn it!"

In 1941, when Hitler was victorious, my mother read Mein Kampf. She kept talking to her lawyer friend about the improvements Hitler had brought to the German people, how great the autobahns were, how strong the Luftwaffe was, how effective their U-boats were, how Hitler had given the Volkswagen to the average citizen, and so on and so forth.

But to all this, my mother's lawyer friend would stop pacing the room and stare my mother and shout, "You haven't read all the newspapers in town, Madame! And how do you know that it is not sheer propaganda? Just wait and see. We are too far away from the scene to know. When this war is over, we will find out the real truth. You will see!"

My mother believed what most of the local population believed, according to the local newspapers, and that was that the people Hitler chose at random to get shot were saboteurs who were blowing up bridges and causing local damage to the rest of the German population. Only after the war had ended would we learn about the serious atrocities committed by Hitler.

Chapter 41

The Best Education

During this period, prefabricated clothing was coming into fashion. One of the first to open such a boutique was Hubert, a wonderful and courteous young man my mother liked and respected, and we often shopped at his store. He looked more like a Scandinavian than one of the local citizens. He was congenial, with a most amiable personality, and his large, bespectacled, myopic, blue eyes searched our faces with comic eagerness.

He had been educated by Jesuit priests and trained for the priesthood or the novitiate but had decided against the monastic way of life to become an import-export dealer in textiles. He sold beautiful dresses and suits, lingerie, children's wear, and other pretty frills and knick-knacks on a fashionable avenue, not too far from a famous hotel where my mother, years earlier, had gone to get a job as a maid but where the hotel owner had, instead, offered to buy personal services from her. Hubert was a Latin and French scholar; his love of business was surpassed only by his love of poetry.

We frequented Hubert's boutique regularly and often stayed to socialize, and since the war news was on everybody's lips at the time, the conversation usually turned to politics. Like my mother's lawyer friend, Hubert believed that the Allies would emerge the victors despite their present, tragic losses. He was confident that the desert war in North Africa was going to be won by General Montgomery.

One afternoon, after we came home from Hubert's shop, I wanted to know what the English were like, as I had never seen an Englishman, except in movies with French subtitles. My mother's reply was, "Well, they are generally tall, slim, and fair-skinned, calm, and they smoke a pipe."

There was a curious look on my mother's face as she told me this. It was hard for me to tell whether she was serious. Within a week after our conversation, the British bombarded the city. Hastily, we made our way to the basement for shelter, such as it was, together with some young French officers who were caught outside during the bombardment.

My mother invited them in and handed us all wads of cotton wool so that we could stuff our ears and shut out the sound of explosions around us. She brought her lute with her into the shelter, as well as a bottle of arak, an alcoholic drink resembling Pernod, or Ouzo, the Greek drink that turns milky white when water is added to it. If we had not been thrown off our seats every so often, and if the blinding explosions had not been too close for comfort, and if the building had not, at times, been shaken to its foundation, anyone would have thought that we were having a party.

My mother seemed unaffected. She played her lute and sang popular songs and handed drinks to everyone. I, however, felt weak-kneed, and I could not stand up, no matter how hard I tried. Even though my mother placed me in the safest corner under a supporting beam, it made no difference. I was sure we were all going to die. But she called the bombs "tennis balls" and said that the British were simply trying to frighten us, without seriously hurting anyone. She repeated the words of one of her many sayings, "Frighten the dog, but don't beat him—that's what the British are doing to us now."

On June 8, 1941, British troops entered Syria from the east and south, forcing the leaders of the Vichy forces and those of the Lebanese, to seek terms. The move discouraged the Germans from attempting to invade the same territories, since they were far too occupied North Africa.

The next day, we went out to see what a British soldier looked like. I remember standing, still a young girl, watching the foreign soldiers in their dusty, khaki uniforms marching in unison. I was so astonished to see that not one of them smoked a pipe. So I turned to my mother and asked, "Maman, not one of them is smoking a pipe. Why?"

Her response was instant. "They can't carry rifles, march, and smoke a pipe at the same time, darling," she smiled.

Hubert was pleased that the British had entered the city. So, too, was our lawyer friend and even my mother. She said she did not care who invaded us, as long as no one was hurt.

What was unusual about her lawyer friend was that his famous house had a gold-plated ceiling and the whole family was more French than French people, it seemed. They all spoke French at home, and many members of the family were educated in France; yet they loved the British.

The famous chief of the Free French Forces, Georges Catroux, promised an end to Syrian occupation and an end to the French mandate in Syria. But when the lawyer brought us the newspaper article announcing the news, my mother would not believe it. She told him that he was being naïve.

"The French had suspended the Syrian constitution in 1939, so how could they now grant freedom to the local population?"

Frustrated beyond words, he took the newspaper and shoved it under her nose. "Look! Look at the date! September 16, 1941! It says here Catroux formally declared Syria's independence and that the Syrian President was fighting for Syria's independence!" He was red in the face and his voice was quite loud.

Every day, he would come and try to prove his point by giving my mother news of yet another German defeat. With a mischievous gleam in his bulging blue eyes, he would read from an Arabic newspaper, translating as he went along, telling my mother that Rommel was losing the desert war, and the hundreds of thousands of Italians had surrendered to the British.

I think that my mother understood Fred more than Fred could imagine. It seemed to be not so much a question of politics, but more a game of psychology. I believe that my mother knew how to treat him. He liked arguments, so she would say almost anything that would make him even more irate. His face would turn red. He would shake his jowls, while my mother would simply smile.

It was perhaps the best first-hand education I ever received, though I might have taken it for granted at the time.

Chapter 42

An Unusual Upbringing

My mother's life seemed to consist of acting, condemned to play different parts, be it at home or on the stage. And despite her fame and influence, she was nonetheless marked by the very nature of her profession. It didn't matter that the whole area was immersed in Egyptian movies and Middle Eastern singers, whose fame had reached as far as France, among them, Umm Kulthum, whom they called "The Star of the East."

I, too, loved all the songs she sang and much enjoyed the music and the acting of stars such as Abdul Wahab, Noor El Hooda, Asmahan, and Farid El Atrash, as well other French, American, and English actors and singers, such as Tino Rossi, Michèle Morgan, Jean Gabin, Betty Grable, Fred Astaire, Robert Taylor, Lana Turner, and dozens of others.

The local theaters were always full with belly dancers and acrobats, as well as performers like my mother who dabbled in all kinds of acting and singing, and there was a slight stigma associated with these professions, especially for my mother as she was one of few women who did not mind showing her legs on the stage or wearing shorts or going cycling, riding a horse, or driving a car, and who was also a single mother, fighting for her survival by openly making use of men.

I lived in a world that was different from that of any other young girl of my age, for I was either doomed or blessed—depending on one's viewpoint—to feel alone, surrounded mostly by men, in a houseful of music and laughter. Yet I was not fully aware of all this until much later in life when I saw families with brothers and sisters and distant relatives and so forth. In a sense, I was kept hostage by the circumstances that had befallen my mother. And it was not until Hubert's existence in our lives that, in a way, I got a brief glimpse of the other side of the local social family life.

Hubert's boutique became sort of a home away from home. My mother and I went there at least twice a week, and eventually, my mother extended her hospitality to the young man. Thereafter, Hubert visited us from time to time, and he was always most welcome. He never came with empty hands, either. He reintroduced me to the poet Sully Prudhomme, whose work Madame Poncelet at the Lycée Français also admired. On another day, Hubert brought me a Cassell's dictionary. Of course, we spoke French all the time. I had studied Armenian and Arabic, a year each, at the Immaculate Conception school, and was given private lessons at home in Turkish, and although my mother and I spoke Turkish and while my Turkish improved with time, I was never as fluent in that language as I would have liked to have been.

One day, Hubert invited me to his house, and if his family did not seem, at first, to object too seriously to the attention he lavished on me, it might have been because they underestimated its depth. The result was that our friendship with him grew unhampered by local traditions or restrictions. Since I had no girlfriends, it was fun to see Hubert and to have him read Sully Prudhomme's poems to me, as my mother had done so often in the past. I felt transported. Later, Hubert introduced me to Jean-Jacques Rousseau and his ideas and Dante's trilogy, which he had read in its original Italian and from which he quoted lines by heart. It was true music to my ears. It seemed to me that the sound of the words was as effective, as musical as their meanings. I was happy to sit and savor every syllable he uttered, for his Italian was excellent, as was his French.

Hubert was one of the few men my mother trusted completely. He was always treated with respect, and, in time, he became like a member of our limited family. With any other man, my mother was cautious, albeit courteous, but I could tell that she was acting a part. They never saw through her; they took her as she appeared: beautiful, cheerful, and welcoming. She carried her wounds like a brave soldier, marching through life bravely, ready for action.

Chapter 43

Coloured Cigarettes, Kidney Stones & Perfumes

My mother did not drink much, other than perhaps half a glass of red wine at the table at lunchtime. Although she did not smoke, she did take the odd cigarette just to please a particular audience when the stage performance was over. She had packets of cigarettes made in Turkey, the likes of which I have never seen since. They were unusually long and narrow; what was amazing about them was that they emitted blue, green, pink, or yellow plumes of smoke. It was like having noiseless fireworks. I would watch some of her friends smoke those fantastic cigarettes, the plumes circling the air like soft, evanescent colorful clouds. They did not emit any of the pungent smell that normal cigarettes did. They were simply puffs of colours traveling the room up to the ceiling and disappearing gradually; it was a real treat for the eyes.

My mother was healthy except that she suffered from kidney stones. The doctor thought it was due to her wounds—the cuts over her back above her kidneys. She drank Urodonal, a pain medication for urinary tract infections, as if it were water. I remember her bringing home an x-ray of her left kidney. She compared it with Carmen Miranda's profile. We laughed at that, but when she suffered excruciating pain, I saw her bite her index finger. I looked at her pain-contorted face with deep concern. Sometimes, she would cling on to Marie and cry with pain.

She also suffered from back pain. She would often have someone come and treat her back with suction cups and massage. These were all caused by the wounds inflected on her back: a hand-carved legacy left to her by my heartless father.

Other than those private moments, the rest of the time she was in charge of her emotions. Perhaps that is why she was such an accomplished actress, both in playing tragic and comic roles.

La Jalousie du Barbouillé, taken from Boccaccio's *Decameron* into Molière's repertoire was a play about a cuckolded and befuddled husband. In this memorable farce, my mother excelled to such a degree as Angélique in that the play was reopened at the same theatre three times in succession.

The set was simple enough. I think the funniest scene included a door, an upstairs window, and the drunk below, if I remember correctly. It seems odd that of all the comedies of Molière, *La Jalousie du Barbouillé* should prove to be such a resounding success. *Tartuffe* or *Le Malade Imaginaire* or any other play did not have the same impact on the audience, as far as I can remember.

I attended the final day of the performance to see my mother receive a standing ovation, bouquets of roses, and deafening cheers. Even when I felt lost among tall people, surrounded by broad shoulders and backs, often unable to see my mother's face or that of any other member of the cast, I applauded fiercely, the palms of my hands burning, my heart thumping with pride.

After the show, my mother and her group would gather at a small, nearby café, famous for its pastry and marvelous ham. At that time of night, the streets were swept clean and washed. I would have a rum ball and a chocolate drink, listening to the comments of the professionals around me. These sessions proved to be invaluable, for I learned more about the subtleties involving acting and actors.

The prompter was a humorous man. He regularly emphasized his importance by telling everybody that, without him, there would be no successful performance. Jokes and laughter mingled with the clicks of coffee cups, but their serious discussions concerned master Molière—the gist being that he was a shrewd observer of humanity, and that he, like Chaucer, debunked the narrow-minded, sanctimonious hypocrites, and that both men were true defenders of *l'amour* in its noblest sense.

When our driver came to pick us up and drive us back home, I sat beside my mother with an incredible surge of pride, smelling the faint, lingering stage make-up, which had become as much part of our lives as her set of fine French perfumes. The fragrance of Eau de Quinine, Lucien Lelong, Coty, and so many others brings back memories of her, just as strongly as do the smells of incense, bleach, urine, and candle wax from time to time bring back the orphanage. It was as if my mother's fine perfumes attempted to suppress or overcome the odors of my wretched early childhood.

Chapter 44

My Mother's Shoe

One beautiful evening, instead of having Maurice drive us as usual, my mother decided to rent a coach, and take a long ride around the city limits. In a coach, she said, she could see the sky, but the car boxed her in. We had taken coach rides before. Most of the time, I preferred jogging alongside the meek emaciated horses that clippety-clopped rhythmically by, instead of sitting inside the coach. As it turned out, this ride was to eclipse all other rides.

Cautious by nature, and because Herunt was busy that evening, my mother asked Ibrahim, a Jack-of-all-trades, to accompany us on our ride. It was getting dark and the presence of a man implied safety.

Ibrahim was a blue-eyed, pale-skinned, Mongolian Muslim, born in Odessa, who had married a Catholic woman named Janette. Ibrahim had been a cook, a jazz musician, and a dancer. In his sixties, he was sprightly but by no means robust, though he was trim and moved about with great agility despite his age. He hardly ever needed a shave, his hairless chest was smooth and white, and his legs could have passed for those of a teenage girl. No wonder he could make us howl with laughter with his female impersonations. He was so much fun that my mother and Uncle paid his fare so that he would accompany us on our summer vacation one year.

That fateful evening in the coach, dressed in his suit of cheap, duck-egg blue, perfectly pressed, with its razor-sharp folds,

Ibrahim made his appearance, with his all-too-familiar, cheap, eau-de-Cologne, which normally wafted in with him and which remained long after his departure. His pale blue eyes sparkling like the summer sky, Ibrahim was his usual chirpy self, full of anticipation for an enjoyable coach ride.

A marvelous breeze ruffled the leaves. The coachman waited patiently, whip in hand, his fez at a rakish angle, his sandaled feet on the side of the wheel, while the horses kept swishing away the persistent flies. We three fitted together on the back coach seat. My mother was wedged in between Ibrahim, seated towards the side of the road, and me, on the other side, closest to the ditch. Once we were settled, the coachman, a half-chewed cigarette dangling from his caked lips, flicked his whip over the horses' heads to start them moving.

We soon found ourselves outside the city, traveling at a good pace, when night fell like a black stone. In that particular part of the world, there were no long sunsets. It was either day or night. We could barely make out the city lights in the distance. The stars sparkled like broken diamonds scattered on a deep purple mantle. Only two cars passed us during all the time we had been moving.

We had been moving for some time when Ibrahim stood for a moment to look at his pocket watch under the coach lamp. It was a little after nine o'clock. He was just replacing his watch when a group of masked men grabbed the horses' bridle and forced the coach to a stop. One brandished a machete knife, another held a revolver to my mother's head. Other masked men surrounded the vehicle, whispering frenziedly among themselves.

It was difficult to distinguish their shuffling shapes among the deep shadows and moonless night, yet my eyes gradually became accustomed to the dark. They were dressed in Mid-Eastern garb; they reminded me of Western highwaymen. I noticed that all seven men were wearing headgear and kerchiefs covering the lower part of their faces. Only the eyes were exposed.

The man holding the gun spoke first, warning my mother that one false move and we were all done for. Two others ordered the coachman to dismount and attempted to swerve the coach to the right, towards the ditch, away from the highway traffic, by madly tugging at the horses' bridles. Suddenly, the coach overturned, and my mother and Ibrahim came tumbling down on top of me. We were miraculously saved by the soft curvature of the ditch, and though we were bruised, no one seemed to be seriously hurt.

The men kept whipping the horses as they tried to get the coach into an upright position, shoving the coachman ahead of everyone else before another car passed by. Once upright and turned onto a dirt road, away from any possible traffic, we were ordered back into the coach. We followed their orders, nervously wondering what they were going to do to us. The bandits still held onto the bridle, pulling the confused horses over what felt like some rough terrain. The coachman, who was receiving rough treatment all the way, kept tripping as he tried to keep pace with the rest of them as ordered. When the men were satisfied with the distance they had put behind us, one of them came forward.

"You! Get off! Get out of the coach! On the double!" he ordered my mother. Even today, I can still see the pair of dark, young eyes behind the checkered kerchief as he stood on the coach step by the faint light. Impatiently, he raised his voice, ordering us off the coach once again.

That was when my mother panicked. She lost all self-control. Weeping and screaming hysterically, she begged the young man to leave me alone, that I was a mere child, an innocent virgin, that she would do anything they wanted, that they could take her life if only they would not touch me. She was pleading with the faceless strangers in a vast, deserted place. All this time, Ibrahim was frozen solid. He neither spoke, nor moved from his seat.

In a harsh tone, one of the men said to my mother, "We are not interested in your ugly child. We want you. Get down. And don't you make a sound!"

My mother leapt down from the coach, telling them in her poor Arabic that, yes, she would do anything for them; at the same time, she frantically tried to reassure me that she would be all right. No sooner had she finished speaking than two men grabbed her and carried her away, her feet dangling in the air. In the shuffle, she dropped one shoe, but she did not seem to care. She kept repeating to me, louder and louder as she got farther and farther away that she would be back soon, that everything was going to be all right.

"Don't worry, Darling! I'll be O.K. Just wait for me. I'll be back soon, very soon!" Her cries became dimmer as they took her away. She disappeared into the dark night. No matter how hard I strained my eyes, I could see nothing. I could not believe what was happening to us. They had taken my mother away. Were they going to bring her back?

Two men kept guard over us, walking round and round the coach, while the coachman quietly waited for further orders. Like a pre-arranged routine, one of the abductors came back to relieve one of the guards, and then, he, in turn, was replaced by yet another newcomer. Each took turns guarding us. I could still see my mother's shoe on the ground nearby, but I dared not make a move to pick it up.

In the distance, we saw the headlights of a passing car, but we were too far away from the main road to attract anyone's attention. After what seemed like ages of sitting speechless and motionless, Ibrahim slowly willed his hand to travel to his pocket to take out his penknife. The first pair, who had now returned to keep an eye on us, looked more relaxed. They were smoking, cupping the lighted ends of their cigarettes in the palms of their hands. Their movements had slowed down, and they'd put their revolvers and knives into their wide sashes.

Ibrahim gave me a careful nudge. I dared not turn my head, but I moved my eyes carefully to look in his direction. In the faint coach light, which was turned away from the road, I saw that he was pointing to the tiny blade questioningly, as if meaning to say, 'Can we do anything with this?'

I shook my head ever so slightly, indicating that he ought to put the thing away. And thank heavens he got the message. All the time I kept wondering what was happening to my mother, why she was not back yet, how had we come to be caught in such a terrible trap. I dared not make the slightest sound or movement. I sat staring into the dark distance, hoping to see my mother again. Teardrops kept falling non-stop down my chin and blouse.

Once again, I noticed Ibrahim was making a move to take something out of his pocket. In my extreme anxiety, believing he was going for his penknife, I jabbed him in the rib as hard as I could, my teeth chattering with fright. I felt conspicuous even in that faint light. I expected one of those men to come and kill us on the spot, and I began to doubt that I would ever see my mother again. I could not stop crying. Then, slowly, while the men were busy talking, Ibrahim showed me the time, making a sign with his fingers to show me that it was two o'clock in the morning. He had taken out his pocket watch, not his penknife.

We'd been sitting there for five hours, yet I felt wide-awake, conscious of the slightest movement or sound. I could hear my heartbeat like a crazy drum. It was like being in a cemetery. The men whispered urgently among themselves now and, from time to time, the horses made a whinnying sound as though they were sneezing. The poor coachman gathered sufficient courage to ask if he could sit down. They told him that he could. As he lowered himself to the ground, a sound of pain escaped from his weary lungs.

At that same instant, Ibrahim and I turned to stare at each other in disbelief. We thought we heard something that sounded like a distant wail or a strange crazy laughter. We thought we heard my mother's voice. Or, were we imagining things? After all, we had been sitting on that coach seat almost all night steeped in anxiety. My eyes felt as though someone had flung a fistful of salt into them.

At long last, the shadows gradually congealed to form the shapes of four men. They were carrying my mother, as if they were shouldering a coffin. The breeze must have carried the sound of her cries long before we were able to make out the moving figures in the distance. They brought my mother to the coach and placed her on the seat as one might a discarded parcel. When I put my arms around her, her shoulders felt sticky and wet. She was bleeding.

I felt the coach once again being pulled away over the stony terrain while the men took turns to whip the poor confused animals. One man, perhaps the leader, walked on ahead, even ahead of the coachman who was being pushed this way and that like his horses over the deserted land.

All of a sudden, we saw the man ahead fall into some sort of a quarry and we heard him cry the name of Allah. It sounded as though he had fallen a long way down and broken his legs. Perhaps he had been killed. I never did find out what happened to that man. The others did not stop to search for him. They simply avoided the danger spot by skirting around the area.

Now there were six men instead of seven, pulling and pushing the coach until they got us back onto the main highway. Before releasing us, they warned the coachman to keep his mouth shut. I heard one of the men say, "Remember, you don't know us, but we know you!"

At that instant, I heard my mother cry out in her most cheerful voice, "Hey, boys! You must come and see me whenever you can. You said you are farmers. Remember you promised to bring me some fresh watermelons! You know where I live!"

Ibrahim and I could not believe our ears. I was flabbergasted that she could speak so jovially to those savages. She went as far as to throw them kisses, as she would to an appreciative audience after a great performance. But, as the coach began, at last, to roll smoothly once again on civilized roads, she began to cry and swear under her breath saying, "Bastards! Oh what bastards!" Then after making sure that we were out of reach, she turned to me and cried, "Darling, did they touch you?"

I told her that no one had come near me. She told Ibrahim and me that all this time she had tried to find some identifying mark so that she would be able to recognize at least one of them, but they gave nothing away; they'd planned the communal rape to perfection.

When we finally got back home, Ibrahim helped my mother take a shower and a douche, put on her bathrobe, and lie down after pulling away the bed covers and telling her to go to sleep.

I lay in bed listening to Ibrahim's voice speaking to me as in a dream. He was saying, "Listen, you don't have to talk. Just remember. No one must know what happened to your mother, not a soul, you understand. I know you can hear me. Just keep your eyes shut and listen, and then I will be off. Your mother would feel terribly disgraced if anyone knew what happened, especially the Judge, whom you call Uncle. No one must know. Remember that. As far as anyone is concerned, your mother fell down the stairs. That's all. You're with me?"

He waited until I whispered a faint "Yes."

"All right now. Go to sleep. You've had a tough day, too. God bless!"

Chapter 45

A Fall Down The Stairs

The following afternoon, Uncle showed deep consternation on hearing the dreadful news, embellished by Ibrahim, about my mother's accidental fall.

My mother was fortunate that he was there when she fell down the stairs, "Otherwise," Ibrahim added, sitting beside Uncle in the living room, now and then throwing a glance at the closed door of my mother's bedroom where she was still sleeping. "Madame would have broken her spine or suffered a concussion if I had not heard someone scream, 'Help me, please! Help me!' I was the last of our band members to walk away because I don't live very far and I enjoy the after-midnight walks. She had just waved goodnight to all of us. Just to make sure, I took out my flashlight and turned towards her place. There she was, lying at the bottom of those stone steps. I found the front door key in her handbag a few feet away from where she lay."

The doctor who came to examine my mother said that she was shaken by the fall, she seemed to have lost a great deal of blood, and was badly bruised, but she would recover. He ordered her to eat parboiled liver at least twice a week, if she could take it, and prescribed antibiotics, ointments, and a mild sedative to help her sleep.

Uncle came every afternoon to visit my mother while she kept to her bed, and he offered to take her on a holiday if she was up to it. He was a loyal and wonderful friend.

When we were alone, my mother said she felt as if she had been trampled over by ten heavy men in hobnail boots. Then she tried to smile and corrected herself: "Or, were there seven?"

She did her best not to worry me, though I knew her body was still quite sore and she was only being brave. But any calm she showed at that time, she lost a few weeks later when the doctor, after another thorough examination, told her that she was pregnant.

Her screams startled us all. "Oh no! There is no respite!"

Ibrahim, who had been paying us regular visits since that terrible day, advised my mother to get an abortion. "Come," he said to my mother, making sure that there was no one around to hear us. "For a few gold sovereigns, you can get rid of the thing. It is done every day."

Eventually, my mother decided to go through with the abortion, but not until we all returned from the mountain resort, for she was still weak and needed to fortify herself for the ordeal. Uncle, however, knew nothing of all this. My mother led him to believe that the baby was his; he had no objection whatsoever to her decision to abort.

Chapter 46

The Cedars Of Lebanon

We stayed at a lovely chalet-like summer resort in Lebanon, and Ibrahim came with us, for Uncle was grateful to him for saving my mother from a worse "fall," as he put it. If it had not been for Ibrahim, the visit might have passed as a more or less ordinary summer holiday, but Ibrahim, with his inexhaustible fund of tall tales, was so diverting, so entertaining, that he made our stay by the gushing, foaming waterfalls, amidst the mountains covered with the famous cedars, a magical event. My mother had invited Ibrahim's wife, but she said she would prefer to stay home because she suffered from motion sickness.

For a while, my mother suffered from mild morning sickness. At first, we four took short walks together, but, gradually, with time, when her appetite grew appreciably in the fresh mountain air, we began to take longer walks up and down its marvelous paths. My mother began to enjoy walking, as each day progressed and we all found the steep climb up the trails more and more invigorating.

We drank ice clear water from shallow streams that murmured peacefully amidst clean rocks. At times, we were driven by hairpin turns where single lanes twisted and turned, where cautious drivers honked and waited, watching the soil slip and crack, taking with it handfuls of stone and rubble miles below to the blue Mediterranean Sea. We went through breathtaking mountain passes, avoiding falling rocks, gasping at the heart-stopping splendor of nature. We filled and refilled our lungs with the scent of pine and cedar. There, it seemed that the world had stopped on its axis. Beautiful peace and quiet, mingled with the crashing of white waterfalls and elusive rainbows.

The curative effects of the wonderful resort soon began to become apparent. My mother became more cheerful, more relaxed and her appetite improved. The swellings, and her aches and pains subsided, and each day brought more color to her cheeks. She went to bed early and, on some days, she slept in.

All this was wrapped in the magical, evergreen paradise of the cedar-clad magnificent panorama. On many mornings, I would stand on our balcony alone, while the others still slept, feeling I could stretch and touch heaven from where I stood, but I was always careful how far I leaned forward for we were thousands of feet up on top of those steep mountains.

In that clean air, I wondered how people could plot to hurt others. What created evil? The world was such a beautiful place, a roofless home for all humanity; yet some people were bound to spoil it. I wanted so much to see my mother well again. She had recovered considerably since our stay at the mountain resort, but her back still gave her some trouble.

Chapter 47

Scheherazade

One evening after supper, as we were sitting on the high balcony of the hotel, nestled among evergreens and foaming waterfalls, Ibrahim was inspired to give us his amusing dissertation on calf liver as the cause of pregnancy. He was inspired by the diet the doctor had prescribed my mother. Ibrahim must have told the story many times, for he seemed to have come prepared. After many repetitions, it must have gathered many embellishments clinging like burrs to the original version.

For the occasion, he had parted his hair sleekly in the middle and put on a white, starched smock, his spectacles, with their half-lenses, resting on the tip of his tiny nose. He referred to a paper in his hand, without once interrupting the flow of his clear delivery, in excellent Turkish, all enlivened by vivid intonation and clever mimicry. His stories had a remarkable positive effect on my mother. He knew it, and he played his part to the hilt. The more my mother chuckled, the better Ibrahim's performance became.

The stars were shining, the blue of the sky looked more velvety. In brief intervals of silence, we could distinguish the gushing sounds of the waterfalls below. They normally drowned the sound of the chirping birds. Swallows by the dozens, in particular, if I remember correctly, darted like black arrows, swooping and swimming silently in the twilight. We could see but not hear them because of the sound of the waterfalls. I loved knowing that we were as lofty as they whenever they swept by our balcony around sunset.

Ibrahim was at his story-telling best when he recounted how he had once impersonated a female belly dancer. We could believe the dancing part, for we knew he could dance well. Indeed, he had helped my mother learn some of the more intricate movements of a specific type of belly dance. But a female impersonation was something else.

He recounted that it was when he was much younger, out of work and hungry, and had one day, drifted into a village by the Caspian Sea, where a stranger asked if he would be interested in taking the place of a female belly dancer who had suddenly taken ill. Ibrahim had jumped at the chance, provided he could be padded in all the right places and veiled so that no one could see his face through the veil. Besides, the money looked good, and he was told he could keep all the money the audience threw on the stage.

So there he was, made up in a smashing costume, along with a lovely silk yashmak. The dress was covered with sequins, the cups of the brassiere were padded, and his head was enveloped in a long wide, semi-transparent red veil hemmed with dazzling artificial gems, and draped over a dusty wig the man had pulled out of an old chest of drawers. Ibrahim decided to call himself Scheherazade and made himself as pretty as he could, using kohl around his eyes, lipstick over his mouth, and powder and rouge on his face.

Before long, he heard the famous Turkish Ciftetelі being played by a four-piece band consisting of a drummer, a violinist, a lutenist, and a nye-player—against the noise of the crowd outside. He fitted his brass hand cymbals on his fingers, adjusted the veil over his blue eyes, and off he went to face the music and the eager audience.

The house was jam-packed with men—women were not allowed out at night in those days—crowded into every available corner, and when Ibrahim stepped forward in his bare feet and heard the shouts of welcome, he began to wriggle his hips and writhe as sensuously as he knew how, trying to keep pace with the drummer frenziedly beating the hell out of his little lap drum. The dance made the cymbals jingle and jangle metallically as he trod round the semi-circular stage with mincing, feminine little steps.

The trouble began when Ibrahim started to revel in the attention he was getting from a giant of a man, whose eyes were glinting with lascivious interest. Carried away by the applause, Ibrahim began to improvise wildly sensuous contortions, even baring his hairless legs up to the thighs as he tried to tantalize with inspired undulations.

What Ibrahim did not realize was that the giant, who sported an enormous mustache which he proudly twirled, was an agha—a military officer—and the richest man in the village, who later appeared at the door of Ibrahim's dressing-room at the end of the second performance, bearing flowers and an invitation for Scheherazade to have supper with him.

The agha, however, had more than supper in mind, and when he tried to touch Sheherazade's breasts, they came off in his hands. Then everything fell apart. The wig came askew, the built-up behind dropped to the floor, and Ibrahim's veil came off, revealing his deception.

The agha turned on Ibrahim with violent anger, swearing to teach him a lesson he would never forget. But Ibrahim, being nimble and light-footed, made a beeline for the door and ran for his life. He heard the midnight train whistle sound in the distance, and as it slowed down for a crossing, he got hold of the moving handrail and hopped aboard.

As we listened to Ibrahim's theatrical story, Uncle would cover my mother's shoulders with her shawl each time it slipped off, for the evenings were becoming quite cool and he was afraid that she would get chilled. We sat on the balcony, with a raffia table in front of us, loaded with all sorts of food.

My mother enjoyed Ibrahim's ramblings, and Uncle was pleased that she seemed happy. He sat as close to her as his moral sense would permit—within touching distance—dying to hold her hand, yet not daring to do so in front of us.

The irony of the whole situation suddenly hit. Here was a wonderful gentleman, a man I had often wished was my real father, a man who dearly loved my mother, and who was too timid to hold her hand in our presence. Yet my mother had been forcibly taken by seven strangers in the middle of one of the largest highways of the city with Ibrahim and myself as cowed witnesses. More than that, Uncle had also been led to believe that he was the father of a child yet to be aborted, which meant that as a judge, he had unwittingly allowed himself to be made guilty of an offense of which he was guiltless. My mother was playing both judge and jury and had foisted on this big-hearted man the responsibility of a heinous act committed by other men, by complete strangers. Uncle was becoming more and more attentive, his devotion increasing with the gradual growth of the child he believed to be his.

What sort of life awaited that unborn baby? I, myself, had lived in spite of unusual odds, in that no one had wanted me at the beginning. My mother did not want to have a child by a man she loathed. My real uncle and grandparents despised me. And I was abandoned at an orphanage without hope of ever seeing my mother again, yet I had lived, and this child was doomed to death before it was born. It was strange. I felt a sudden pain squeeze my heart. That baby could have become my sister or my brother, but it would never know me. It would never know its real father. If my mother allowed the baby to live, it would grow up, like me, wondering who its father was. And Uncle was nobody's father, and nobody's husband, for that matter. I found it all so puzzling.

Chapter 48

The Baby In Formaldehyde

A few weeks later, we were back home. And on the day my mother had to have her abortion, I felt sick at heart. I could not allow her to kill that baby—no matter whose it was. I clung to her at the door, trying to stop her from going. But she went anyway. When it was all over, when she came back home a few hours later, she looked pale and tired. With a gesture quite typical of her, she showed me a bottle she was carrying. Inside was the figure of a nearly perfectly formed body—that of a boy—preserved in formaldehyde. I stared at the wizened, eyeless head. She, too, was quite shaken. She said that this creature was the son of one of those men who had raped her, "But," she asked, "How could we have told Uncle about it?"

I took the bottle, crying out that he was, nevertheless, my dead brother and that she had killed him. I had never before spoken so sharply to my mother, and I regretted it at once. But it was too late to take it back.

"It was not our fault for having been born where we were or who we happened to be," she said. "No one can choose his or her fate. We are born somewhere. Something happens. It can happen to anyone. No one chooses this sort of life. It is not my fault that I was forced to marry your father, a man I had never seen before. Being forced to go to bed with a stranger, especially one you don't like at first sight, is close to being raped, darling." As she spoke, I knew I'd hurt her with my cutting words, but, as was her style, she was teaching me a lesson. I felt ashamed.

"Just an innocent coach ride and this is what happened. We cannot change it. But we can try to forget it. People on the whole are good, sweetheart. I believe that. Some spoil it. The world is a beautiful place, it is some people who ruin it."

She took me in her arms. She looked so weak, so frail. I was sorry I had said those awful things to my Maman. I had reproached her for the fact that she had led Uncle to believe that it was his child. Again, with the same calm detachment, she said that there was no other way to explain her pregnancy.

"At least you are intact, my darling," she said as calmly as she could manage. "And you shall remain so for as long as I live. My life is over, darling, but I have you to live for, and that is the most important thing in the world for me. I want to see you get married and have children. But before that, I want you to study hard and get somewhere in this world. I want you to get your Bracelet of Independence. That way, you can work, earn your living by honest means, and do what you want in a free world. As you know, that's my dream. Study hard, darling. Education is your best friend."

Chapter 49

Too Many Questions

Uncle took the news of my mother's abortion well. He congratulated her on the strength of her character. As I stood on the outside, looking in with a broken heart, I was struck by a new kind of irony. Uncle was commending my mother for freeing him of the responsibility, which he believed to be partially his own, but was he also commending her for her complicity in the dreadful solution? Whether it was his child or not, was he not involved in the decision, and was I right in absolving Uncle altogether? Indeed, what nobility had I ever seen in this man? It could not have been his regular loyal visits to our house, for there were many others like him; many who came regularly, many who gave my mother more money than he did. He was prepared to make love to her every night. He never hurt her feelings. He was always courteous and attentive. He even dared show his face at the theatre one night when he was concerned about her health.

My mind was teeming with questions. What made Uncle so special? Was it his intense love of her, and if he did really love her, why did he not marry her? And why did he pay her clandestine visits? Why did he never invite her to his own house, to meet his mother and sister? Was he a trustworthy person or just clever? Might he be just like one of those seven men in the way he came regularly to ravish her under the guise of affection? What was the difference between an open rape and Uncle's devious seductions after I went to bed? Was he not perhaps trying to protect his immaculate reputation?

The only difference I could see was that the seven men were armed, whereas Uncle's weapons lay in his fame and power, his influence as an honest judge. But how honest was a judge who crept about at night because he was afraid of being seen with my mother? Could one love someone or something they were ashamed of?

I could not help connecting these troubling questions with the little I knew about the circumstances of my own birth. When I asked my mother why we had come to Aleppo from Turkey instead of, for instance, going to Europe, she explained that it was closer, and anyway, we could not have moved to Europe without permission from the authorities. She was born in Turkey. We could have visited Europe but not lived there.

But then, struck by another idea, I asked her why we had to run away from the city I was supposed to have been born in. Did it have anything to do with my father? This is when my mother became a little impatient. "Please, darling," she said, "please, don't open up old wounds. Give me time to recover from the new ones. You know I hate discussing your father." She then picked up a book and pretended to read it.

I shouted, "I am like that baby in the bottle of formaldehyde, aren't I?" To this day, I don't know what made me say it, but I did.

She snapped the book shut, frowning, and turned to look at me.

"After all," I went on, "my father raped you, in a sense. You hated him and you were forced to marry him and then you had me, and so you must have hated him as much as you hate those seven men who raped you!"

Suddenly, I went flying to the floor, my mother standing next to me. In a voice as hard as steel, she warned, "Never! Never say that again. You know how much I love you—you saw me give myself that night to those bastards so that they would not touch you. Never, and I mean never, for as long as we live, will you ever mention your father to me again!"

Chapter 50

Fate Favours The English

Early during the Second World War, many Armenians began leaving for Soviet Armenia. Of the eighty thousand Armenians in the city where we lived, many were encouraged to go to Yereven or Erevan, in Soviet Armenia, tempted by the promise of a homeland, among whom were some of the dearest and nearest to my mother and me.

When my mother read about the emigration in the local newspapers, she said she wished that they would not go. When I asked her why, she told me that it was better not to trade the sour cream you've tasted to the cream that you have not. Also, she felt hurt that Nevart's only daughter was leaving for the new Armenia. Elias, too, decided to go, and so did precious Barkev, her violinist. It was hard for my mother to see these friends leave forever, and at such short notice. Both Barkev and Elias had broken the news just a few days before leaving, and it had come as a shock to my mother. She was fond of them, but they left with our heartfelt good wishes.

We continued to follow the evening radio broadcasts with great interest, especially the nine o'clock news from London, England, announced by the chimes of Big Ben and the infamous Lord Haw-Haw. While I hesitate to show happiness related to war, I did enjoy the lively arguments that flared up in our living room during the war years. Fred was right about the desert war at El-Alamein and became even cockier, telling my mother that British Spitfires and Hurricanes had won the Battle of Britain.

One day, when my mother and I were alone, she told me that victory did not last forever. "It seems," she said, "even great empires crumble, darling." She reminded me of the great Roman Empire, how their famous military leaders had proved to be great conquerors; yet even that empire crumbled eventually.

"One glaring example would be Julius Caesar—his triumphant march to Rome, his crossing of the Rubicon, his presence in Syria, where he said, 'Vini, vidi, vici', meaning, 'I came, I saw, I conquered', because he found it so easy to conquer. He also controlled Britain and Gaul."

My mother's attitude towards the British became more and more positive. The more we saw of them, the more we liked them. The English left a lasting impression on our lives because of my brief contact with the people at the American College. Thanks to my teachers there, I fell in love with the English language. It was also the place where I learned an object lesson in working with others.

Chapter 51

Learning Things In Life

At the American College, students took turns cleaning the blackboards, tidying up the chairs and desks, and sweeping the floors. I did not realize that I had to take part in this routine until one of the teachers stopped me after class, just as I was about to leave for home.

I liked my teacher, for she encouraged me in my study of English; because of this, and my mother's belief that English was going to be the most important language in the world, my English improved considerably within a short period of time. I practiced it every day and did my homework with great love and dedication. I even showed some of my poems to my teachers for their approval, all of whom encouraged me to continue to write.

On that day, however, my teacher held out a broom for me with a dust cloth. She explained in her gentle manner that it was my turn to pitch in with the work. I knew that some girls from wealthy families did not mind helping out, but I felt so outraged that I told her that if she needed someone to clean the school, I would be happy to ask my mother to send our servant, Marie, to do the work.

"I am not at an orphanage," I said haughtily. "We pay for our education at this school."

She did not become angry. She merely asked me to wait by the door while she did the sweeping so that the other students would not notice that I was unwilling to do any work that they had had no objection to doing. So I stood by, watching my teacher clean the classroom.

After a few minutes, I felt ashamed of myself. Here was my teacher doing the work I had refused to do so that I would save face. Embarrassed, I asked her to allow me to finish the work. I told her that I was sorry and that I had not understood the significance of the routine. I pleaded with her to let me do the rest of the work. Finally, she smiled and handed me the broom.

"I'll be in my office if you need me. Don't worry," she said, "we all have to learn things in life. It is good to learn." She smiled and left. That was a lesson I did not mind learning, for it reinforced, once again, the symbolic meaning behind the photograph of Anush and of myself hanging on the wall in my bedroom.

Chapter 52

Countries: Prisons Or Bastions Of Freedom?

Even though there was a great deal of German propaganda in that part of the world, most of the visitors at our house who took a great interest in world affairs seemed optimistic that, with the help of the United States, the British would end up victorious.

When the British entered the city in 1941 and I was about 13 years old, some occupied a block not too far from where we lived. What impressed us was the courteous manner of the New Zealanders who greeted us each time we passed their headquarters. They always stopped to say hello. As we shared the same sidewalk, we could not avoid witnessing their morning and afternoon drills when we happened to be out.

One of the soldiers, Bill, soon became a friend. He became a regular visitor at our house and began to call me his little sister. He made us promise that someday we would go to New Zealand to meet his girlfriend and his parents, and though we never did, we corresponded for many years thereafter. We even received a piece of the wedding cake when Bill got married. He was a decent person.

It seems strange when I look back now that it took a New Zealander to open our house to the English in general. We soon found ourselves hosts to soldiers and officers from Australia and all parts of England. All this time, I tried to speak as much English as I could, while my mother struggled to remember what little English she had studied in her native city of Adana.

I wanted to attend university somewhere in Europe but had not decided exactly where; more importantly, the cost was still to be considered. I asked my mother how I would be able to afford university if she did not have the money to do it.

"I hope to be able to save enough money, and, after that, you just keep working hard at whatever university you happen to land at, and write, by all means. Keep writing poetry. You seem to love doing that. But that will not earn you much bread, sweetheart. You need a profession. By the time the war ends, I will have fleeced all the men I know. I've saved quite a bit, but nowhere near enough to last you several years at a university somewhere abroad, not yet anyway. Things are a bit tight these days but, with care, we should be able to manage to send you to Geneva. And it looks as if the end of the war is not too far away. We pray that it ends soon, sweetheart."

As a young girl, I often saw my mother count gold sovereigns and slide them off the tabletop into her lap with a smile. Her wardrobe was filled, not only with magnificent clothes, but also with gold coins and paper money. Rolled-up banknotes by the thousands would lie at the bottom, by her shoes and slippers, later to be converted at the bank into English gold currency. She still believed in the value of gold, and, like most people she knew, she converted everything she could into gold and hoarded it, keeping paper money for everyday use.

In spite of the war and the occasional economic shortage, I never felt that we were short of funds. I always had enough money in my pocket because my mother insisted that I never go short again. The shops could be closed for a few days, but my mother always knew someone who could find her anything we needed.

Yet she began to rely more and more on Uncle and Fred for financial support. She went on the occasional brief tour with her band, but the concert engagements were fewer than before.

The thought that one day I might study in Europe somewhere excited me so much that I buttonholed Fred next time he came to our house. I knew that a close member of his family had studied in Paris.

"Isn't the University of Paris called the Sorbonne, and isn't it supposed to be one of the best universities in the world?" I enquired. "Can I go and study and live there?"

"Of course it is, but this is where we live. You can't pick up lock, stock, and barrel and just go and live wherever you wish."

"Why not?" I challenged.

I caught my mother's glance, but she said nothing. Fred's thick bushy eyebrows rose as I repeated, "Why not, Fred?"

"Because you cannot simply choose a particular part of the globe and decide to go and live there," he huffed.

Again, I pushed for an explanation. "Why?"

He got up to pace the living room, using gestures he adopted when arguing with my mother. "As you might have learned in school," he went on slowly, "the world is divided into countries, and each country has its own laws. We can study or take a holiday abroad somewhere, if we are fortunate enough—that is, if we have the funds—but we cannot go and live there simply because we decide to do so."

Fred's answer disappointed me. "So, in a sense, every country can be a prison for all those born in it," I replied.

"It can be, but it can also be a liberator of thought—a promise of freedom and democracy. Like England, for instance, or France, or any other country."

"Why?"

"Because those countries have already been through the dark ages. It has a great deal to do with political leaders. For one example, women can vote in England. The suffragettes did a super job there and in other places too."

Fred stopped pacing the room when he saw Marie with the customary cup of coffee. He took the cup and thanked her and sat down smiling whimsically at her. Meanwhile, my mother was busy reading an Armenian newspaper Fred had brought her.

Fred nursed his cup, sipping from it every so often while responding to my never-ending questions, patiently enough, though with a strange smile on his lips.

Suddenly, my mother's voice was heard from behind the newspaper, "In England, and in many parts of the world, the role of women differs considerably, darling," she said and folded the newspaper looking at me. "For instance, there is polygamy here, a man can have many wives— which is fine and there is a good reason for it. In ancient times, men went to war and women or young girls were left behind. This was one way of solving the population problem. The tradition was borrowed from earlier times, for example, King Solomon, the great king who is respected by all other religions, had a huge harem. That way, married men didn't have to deceive their wives, for instance, or resort to divorce procedures. Anyway, women in Europe can work alongside with men today. There are several ways of looking at anything. I don't criticize men who prefer to work and have their wives stay at home. I think that is commendable, especially when we read about the divorce rates rising in many parts of the world. Besides, if a woman insists on working, the children might suffer because the offspring comes home from school to find an empty house or the parents have to pay a babysitter. Nothing can replace the presence of a mother in a home. Who are we to say, darling? Every household is able to decide whatever it wishes to do. All I want is to be allowed to give you the education you need so that you can decide for yourself, sweetheart, that's all. We'll have to wait for the end of the war and see what happens."

At the mention of war, Fred seemed to reengage in the conversation. "The Americans are now sending supplies and forces to England," he told us. "I read it in the newspaper recently. Soon they will get caught up with the war. Once they do, there goes the mighty Hitler!"

My mother did not respond. "According to this," he added excitedly, pointing to the newspaper he was holding, "the U.S banned all trade with Japan. How about that? On top of that, Japan is at war with China. She can't possibly assist Germany, can she?" he asked.

My mother said, "You are reading into things. Let me see that paper. Japan is still neutral towards Germany. Where did you read it says Japan and Germany are allies?" She pulled the newspaper from his hand, but she put it aside when she saw that it was in Arabic, because she could not read Arabic.

Fred went on, "You must be aware that Japan and Russia are old enemies. Now, with Russia on the side of Britain, Germany will turn to Japan. It is logical."

I was not able to follow any of their political discussions or arguments. All I could do was to listen and be quiet. My own questions, only partially answered, seemed forgotten.

Fred's political prophecies soon came true. After Russia joined the western allies and Japan brought the United States into the war, the long fight for the liberation of Europe began. I grasped some of the political history years later. At the time, it held little significance, except for the fact that I, like everybody else, hoped to see the end of the war. For a while, matters seemed to improve. There was more stability in our part of the world as the local riots subsided, and, by the middle of 1944, the French decided to hand over all administrative and legislative functions to the Syrians.

We got most of the daily war news from the radio broadcasts, and our newspapers, of which there were at least ten different ones, but we rarely wondered whether these were tampered with or altered to suit their various sources and their points of view as the course of the war turned in favor of the Allies.

Armenians, Jews, and other ethnic minorities had little power in local politics or current affairs, according to Fred. The majority population was pushing for its independence. As a result, members of the minority groups tended to conduct their business as quietly and as honestly as they could without committing themselves to any particular cause. Shopkeepers, my mother commented proudly, were advertising their wares in Arabic, French, Armenian, Greek, or Hebrew, and they all lived peacefully, side by side. While out buying nuts one day, I saw evidence of this firsthand, spotting one shop sign written in Hebrew and the one next to it written in Arabic or Greek.

In spite of the so-called Syrian independence achieved on January the first in 1944, the French and English troops did not leave Syria until about two years later.

Chapter 53

Half-Finished Ice Cream

When Hosanna was not on tour performing, she and I fell into the habit of strolling the streets to take an ice cream at a nearby café.

It was just on such an unbearably hot summer evening while my mother and I were lingering over our ice cream that a complete stranger, about thirty and in uniform, approached our table to ask if he might join us. My mother explained that she preferred not to be seen in public with men in uniform, if only in deference to local customs. The stranger showed no surprise. He excused himself and left.

It was an odd occurrence. We had never set eyes on the soldier before, and, as far as we knew, he was not one of our British neighbors down the road. Besides, he had put his foot on one of the empty chairs as he had bent over to speak to us, which was not at all the customary thing to do while addressing ladies. We soon dismissed him from our minds, and enjoyed our lazy summer evening, sitting and watching people go by. The sidewalks of the city were packed with pedestrians strolling along, all hoping for a cool breeze. As usual, the summer was long and hot and dry.

A few days later, at the same café, the same scene repeated itself, as if the first one had been a mere rehearsal. Again, my mother refused to let the stranger sit at our table. He pointed out that there were other local citizens sitting with British soldiers and that he simply wished to talk to us. My mother looked around, and, indeed, there were many British officers and soldiers sitting with local people of both sexes, but she feared for my reputation. It was then that she pronounced one of those perhaps fatal and irrevocable sentences: "All right, but only for a few minutes."

The noise around us suggested a happy place. I could hear English and local languages being exchanged in a loud and lively manner, interspersed with laughter. I was dressed in a white cotton dress with a flared skirt and white sandals. It was a day not to soon be forgotten, for it would alter the course of our lives.

I noticed the stranger's graying temples as he took off his cap and placed it on his knee. His features gave him an unusual bearing. He had some medals pinned on his khaki uniform. He was tall and thin, and his eyes were the color of brandy, not unlike the color of my mother's eyes.

My mother waited graciously enough. Her pale green suit and fern-green shoes, handbag, and straw hat offered a beautiful coolness to our table.

"You must forgive me, Madame…" He hesitated for a second, and then stopped.

"Yes?" my mother asked. She looked sorry for the stranger.

The stranger tried to explain awkwardly, "You see, Madame, I know who you are. That is, I have seen you and your daughter here a few times from the balcony of my office, which is not far from your house. And I followed you here a few times before I dared to introduce myself to you."

My mother and I looked at each other in surprise. We did not remember seeing that person before. He took in our brief exchange of glances. Something far more than casual curiosity, far deeper than a simple need for company, seemed to flow out of his words. There was a certain resonance of deep sincerity and sadness at the same time.

To break the silence, my mother ventured, "And what is your name, sir?"

"Abraham," he responded looking at me intently.

"What do you wish to say to us, Abraham?" my mother asked softly.

"This will probably take you by surprise, Madame, but, may I invite your beautiful daughter out for dinner?" he asked.

I could hardly believe that the man was referring to me as beautiful. No one ever had.

"I am sorry, Abraham, my daughter cannot go out with anybody. Now please be good enough to leave."

He turned and looked at me once more with a hurt expression, holding me steadily with his soft gaze. Then he said, "au revoir," and left. My mother and I watched his tall person move away with elegant, measured pace.

"He did not finish his ice cream," I said.

"I feel he'll be back to finish it someday soon, darling," she responded.

Chapter 54

Education As A Liberator

That same evening, we came back to the house to find Nevart's husband, Kevork, in our living room waiting for us. Nevart was my mother's best friend; Nevart's daughter had left for Armenia with other Armenians; and her son had been shot in a skirmish a few years earlier.

Kevork was a quiet, nondescript sort of a man, of no great intellect, in direct contrast to Nevart, his wife, who was endowed with a keen mind although uneducated in the normal sense of the word. He polished rusty pots and pans for a living, working with a special sort of a kiln in the artisans' quarter in the famous market. I had been there a number of times for various reasons; to me, it possessed some sort of magic, dating back to the 12th or 13th century. Their vaults shielded the sun, trapping the cool air that rose after the local merchants watered the sandy cobblestones every afternoon to keep the dust down.

I remember the sure-footed sherbet-sellers bending down to pour out cups of delicious sherbet for thirsty pedestrians, using and re-using the same communal metal cup dangling from a chain attached to the huge pot of sherbet. I know just how tasty that dark brown liquid could be.

Each section in the marketplace consisted of ranges of shops and stalls where Kevork worked.

The jewelers' quarter, where Karnik made my mother's specially-designed jewelry, was unequalled in its silver filigree workmanship. In the same area, gold was bought and sold in a thriving black market. Beyond the jewelers' quarter, a warren of cool and narrow paths led to the brass and leather workshops where Kevork worked, then to the dealers in spices and silks.

In the cafés, men of all ages sat around on low rattan chairs, playing tric-trac or dominos as they contentedly sucked at their narghiles, while others sipped thick, black coffee in tiny brass cups.

Under impromptu canopies of richly hued silks stretched from one street corner to the other to dry in the sun, workers in bare feet or loose sandals lazed on huge bales of cotton, awaiting customers with an air of sublime confidence. Bales of cloth of all colors rested in rows in the backs of shops that could be padlocked at the end of each hot, busy day.

Inside display windows, or on the rough ground outside, cheap trinkets were lined up to tempt buyers. It was a confusing profusion of Middle Eastern clothes, sequined soft scarves, belts, purses, slippers, shoes, sandals, famous Damascene silks or inlaid mother-of-pearl, low, octagonal coffee tables, brass trays, coffee pots, and clay pots by the dozen.

Donkeys, goats, dogs, cats, children, and carts all somehow managed to get through the busy, narrow, shaded streets. The poor donkeys did more work than the people there. They were overloaded with boxes and bags and sacks of all sorts. They were so encumbered that the animals themselves could hardly be seen. They were whipped each time they stopped or goaded with sharp sticks heartlessly jammed into their flanks.

Nevart hadn't visited us recently, and we missed her cheerful face and ready wit. That is why we felt some alarm at Kevork's presence, for he rarely left his work. He explained he was worried about his wife—she'd contracted tuberculosis and was now bed-ridden, coughing up blood. Kevork looked worn out as he pleaded with my mother to go and visit his wife. He kept wiping his eyes every so often and staring silently in our direction.

Unlike other merchants who either bartered tirelessly, fanning themselves furiously with bits of paper, or those who sat back indifferently waiting for customers, Kevork, no longer a young man, was hard at work polishing old pots and pans and trays, using hard physical energy in an overheated shop. He worked from dawn till dusk to earn the pittance that went towards their wretched existence and to pay the heavy medical bills for his wife's illness. Sadly, it was cheaper to die quickly.

After a hectic taxi ride, as Maurice was attending his daughter's wedding that day, we reached Kevork's house on the other side of town. My mother ran ahead of us to the bedroom where Nevart lay. Kevork followed slowly, as if he were carrying all the metal pots and pans of the world on his frail old shoulders. He seemed unable to will his legs to move any faster. He plodded along, despair paralyzing every one of his gentle gestures.

When I came into the bedroom, I saw my mother leaning over to hug her best friend, but Nevart shook her head violently, pushing her away with her bony hands. Her parted lips were bloodied. She had a large metal bucket beside her bed. All the windows were wide open although it was a cool September evening. When she saw me looking at her, she told me in a weak voice to sit over by the door so that I would not come in close contact with her.

She forced herself to speak. She spoke of dying, and, as she spoke, she brought up spittle stained with blood.

"I only have that simpleton of a husband to cry over me and you, my dearest friend," she said, spitting blood into the bucket.

We were all saddened. Nevart was still a young woman, not yet forty-seven; yet she was aching for the peace of death.

Kevork's huge empty hands with the broken fingernails rested on his soiled gray shiny trousers. His work boots were worn and dirty.

Nevart gestured towards him. "What about that poor idiot?" she said, "Who will look after him when I'm gone?"

She seemed exhausted but wanted so much to talk. It was as if she was going on a trip and was desperately trying to get all the last-minute instructions off her chest. She rambled on, while we wept for her feeling helpless.

"I'm lucky," she said between bouts of choking and coughing. "I'm lucky, but you have to suffer." And looking directly at me, she said, "Remember this. Are you listening?"

I was hanging on to every word she was able to get out, and those words still echo in me today. "Look after yourself and never let anyone take advantage of you."

I shook my head, unable to speak.

"Your mother is doing all she can to save you from the kind of life she is trapped in. So be good and work hard at school. Concentrate. Okay?"

She started to cough up blood again—so much, she nearly choked. Her handkerchief dripped with blood.

This time, my mother could bear it no longer. "Stop talking, Nevart! You can hardly breathe. Relax!" And then she handed Nevart her own handkerchief, taking the used one and throwing it into the bucket.

But Nevart would not stop, as if she had some terribly urgent message to convey. She went on for most of the evening while we listened helplessly. She called my mother one of the living dead and urged her to save me because I was young enough to survive. She kept repeating,

"She mustn't end up like you…or me, for that matter. Sure, I have a husband, but look at my life! My eight-year-old son was killed by a stray bullet during a riot in which none of us was involved. And now my beloved daughter left for Armenia hoping to make a new life for herself. What happens to that poor idiot of a husband, over there? Tell me!"

She went into a paroxysm of coughing and vomiting more blood into the handkerchief she held to her mouth. Suddenly, she gasped for breath and let her head fall back on the soiled pillow.

We could distinguish her bony frame and skinny legs under the sheets. She looked ninety years old. Her eyes were closed, but her bloodstained mouth fell open. She lay there, pale and wrinkled, her long, curly, brown hair spread over the pillow.

All this time, her husband made no move except to raise his blank eyes to look at his wife; it was as if, he, too, were dying.

Chapter 55

An Accident Of Geography

For many nights after Nevart's death, I found it difficult to fall asleep. I could still see Nevart's face and her emaciated body lying there, helpless, coughing blood and I could hear her rasping voice when she called my mother one of the living dead, while pleading, in her last breath, to rescue me from the kind of life I might face. She reminded me of Marie's mother, lying on the divan cold and silent like a statue. Perhaps because I had seen Nevart from time to time, her final words left a deep impression on me, if not her demise.

As sleep evaded me, I could not help thinking of my future and Fred's explanation that one had to remain in one's place of birth for life, regardless of the country where one acquired one's education. I knew I could not practice law, even if I managed to go to a university somewhere abroad, even if my mother managed to pay for it. We'd never seen a woman lawyer in the city where we lived.

Perhaps, I thought to myself, I could become a midwife, but that did not appeal to me much. I could not have become a teacher or a professor because all the female teachers at the Lycée Français were forced out of the country during the local uprising against the French. I felt confused. And if I did go abroad, and never returned, what would happen to my mother?

Tears began to blind me. I put on the lights, picked up a book from the bookshelf beside me, sat down on the bed, having arranged the pillows comfortably behind me, and began to read. Every so often, I'd wipe my eyes, blow my nose, and continue to read.

During the following three months, my mother was always at the theatre at least until one o'clock in the morning, so she was not aware of my restless nights. I spent several sleepless nights in this way.

I kept telling myself that it was simply a question of geography and patches of land that stood in my way. Look at Bill, I reminded myself, the British soldier who had become our friend and who had invited my mother and me to his wedding in New Zealand, and who had later enclosed a picture taken with his fiancée in front of a lovely house and garden. But it was in New Zealand. In Auckland! It was several thousands of miles away, on the other side of the world. It went without saying that we would never be able to make the trip, but why was I condemned never to see the other side of the world just because I was born on this side of it? Somehow, Nevart's death and Bill's wedding seemed irreconcilable opposites: Death on one side, a new life on the other, with me suspended in between—alive, yet trapped by an accident of geography.

Geography created enemies even in peace time, for, as Fred had explained, no one could just leave one patch of land, marked, for instance, *France*, to go to another part marked *Germany*. Yet, Bill, who had fought his way into our part of the world with bombs and bullets, would likely have been refused entry if he had decided to move to our area as an ordinary citizen. The whole thing seemed ridiculous. Wasn't this supposed to be God's world, and were we not all human beings—citizens of this globe?

Despite my sleepless nights, I attended classes as usual, not bothering to hide my swollen eyelids and blood-shot eyes. Nevart lay buried in my heart, but her memory was to stay with me longer than I had realized.

Chapter 56

Broken Childhood

One evening before going to the theatre, my mother came to my bedroom to announce that she'd planned a trip for me. When I heard that she was going to send me a long distance away, I wondered whether she had decided, after all, to send me to New Zealand, to attend Bill's forthcoming wedding. But I was mistaken. She was going to send me to Iskenderun, or Alexandrette, as the French called the port that was now ceded by them to Turkey.

"Why Iskenderun, Maman?" I asked wild-eyed.

She explained that it was because she had dreamt of my grandmother, whom I vaguely remembered as being a gentle, lovely woman who lived with my cross-eyed and equally cross-tempered uncle, Johannes.

My mother looked uncomfortable. She fumbled with her handkerchief, desperate to speak of something that must have moved her deeply. For the first time, I sensed the sad little girl buried deep down within her. Finally, she explained that the dream had brought vivid scenes about her own early days with her family in Adana and later in Alexandretta, so now she wanted me to go and visit my grandmother there.

I rarely saw my mother lose control. Even when she was raped in the woods that awful night, she maintained control. But now, her shoulders shook as she buried her face in her handkerchief and wept. Then she said, looking at me with all the love in the world, "I have to go and perform soon, sweetheart.

But the scene is etched in my memory. I was younger than you are now. I remember sitting in our car with my parents on our way to the Armenian Orthodox Church in Adana. Because my father—that is your grandfather, darling—had bought the first Ford motorcar in the city, all the neighbors came to admire it. Oh, I was so proud of my parents!" She stopped and sniffled. I felt transfixed. My mother did not believe in crying in front of anyone. Perhaps Nevart's death had affected her more than we could have imagined.

She continued: "My father looked so pleased and my mother looked so lovely. Johannes, my brother, was just a child then, but for some reason he sat sullenly beside me saying nothing. The dream was so real, I remember what I was wearing then: My dress, my shoes, my gloves and my new hat. I…" She could not continue. She grasped my arm, almost shouting. "Where have those days gone, darling?"

I had often watched my mother in tragic roles on the stage, but this sudden and disarming scene in my bedroom left me numb. She tried to force herself to smile and took my hand.

"Gloves and shoes are a bad sign in dreams. They mean more worries. Your uncle was dressed in his Sunday suit. He looked so cross, yet so handsome!" She wailed. "All this happened because of your father. Your grandfather killed himself because he could not face the disgrace. He forced me to marry a man I had never seen before. I was just a teenager, darling! And look at us now!"

"I didn't know that my grandfather had killed himself," I said, surprised.

"I tried to spare you the pain, darling," she responded, her beautiful face contorted with anguish. She made a poor attempt to smile, but the smile died on her lips. I bent and kissed her wet cheek. She looked tired and vulnerable. It was so unlike her ever to break down or show that much heartbreak.

She spoke again without looking at me, her eyes fixed on some distant thought or some past joy that made the present all the harder to bear. She stood up, getting ready to leave for the theatre, and sighed a long deep sigh. "Ah! It's been so many years!"

My mother kissed me good night, saying, "I'll be fine, darling, don't fret. We've been through worse. Try to sleep."

But, again, I could not sleep. Instead, I pictured my grandmother—her chubby face and her petite figure standing before me as large as life. She had long chestnut hair rolled into a bun and stuck at the nape with a large hairpin. And I could see, as on a dark screen, my real uncle, Johannes, and almost reading the dislike he harbored in his heart for me. I felt his huge fist pounding the small of my back.

I saw myself squatting on the dirt ground, washing an endless number of demitasses of Turkish coffee. I must have been no more than two years old at the time, but it was clear and sharp. In the same flash of memory, I also saw a low-hanging wide wooden door opening slowly, and as I entered, I could just make out to my left the outline of a banana tree. To my right, I saw a broad expanse of garden with fig and persimmon trees and others whose names I never learned. Closer to the entrance, and a little to the right, stood the circular stone wall of the water-well.

And I saw the house proper, a large bungalow with windows of the living room wide open, where someone was playing the mandolin. The haunting tune faded away like a shadow.

In another niche of memory, I saw large slabs of smoothly cut stones resting one on top of the other. I saw a tall, skinny man with a hooked nose and a large mustache lifting a sizable rock with a crowbar to expose a family of slithering poisonous snakes, while a disembodied male voice warned that the reptiles were poisonous, that the skinny man ought to be careful.

Superimposed on those broken images was the terrifying fall of the skinny man from a tall ladder.

Were these visions based on some actual events that I had suppressed? Had I really seen that house or had I imagined it? Or had my mother lied to me? Had I been born outside my birthplace, the city where we were living now? Perhaps I was born in Iskenderun when it was still part of Syria? That would account, perhaps, for my earlier memories of the place.

In a split second, I came to the incredible realization that I knew exactly what to expect in Iskenderun, once I got there. It was because I had been there before. My mother had told me that she had run away from Iskenderun with me in order to get away from my uncle and the bad treatment we were both getting from her parents. If we ran away together from Iskenderun to Aleppo, how come I was registered as being born in Aleppo before we got there? She didn't have the answer. None of it made sense. To this day, it does not make any sense.

For whatever reason, I had never been admitted into all of my mother's past life, though now and then I might have been given a glimpse of a disturbing past, floating in my subconscious memory like an unpleasant image somewhere in the back of my child's mind. But no matter how hard I tried to dust it off and bring it out into the sunlight, the shapes remained ill-defined and confusing.

It was with the scarcely realized intent to know more of these long-forgotten incidents that I packed my small suitcase and prepared to leave.

The dream had so affected my mother that she was still disturbed the following morning while we waited for Maurice to come round with the car. I could do nothing to lighten her mood, for she feared that her mother, after all these years, would still not have forgiven her for our running away.

In the harsh bright sunlight, Marie and my mother looked

old and tired. Marie handed me a bag of sandwiches and my wool jacket. "You will need these, Mademoiselle," she said gently, trying to smile.

I was carrying with me the letter my mother had written to my grandmother and to my uncle, as well as the gifts she had bought for them. When she kissed me goodbye, I began to feel I was on my way back not only to Iskenderun, but into my past; that I would soon be able to put back together some of the pieces of my broken childhood.

Chapter 57

The Drive To Iskenduren

Once Maurice and I were on the road, I could hardly contain my excitement. I was about to confirm whether the place I saw in my mind's eye really existed. We ate our chicken sandwiches while he drove, and I watched the scenery roll by.

We left the flat desert land behind and started climbing up into mountains. Once, we turned to the right so sharply I had to cling to the car seat with both hands, too scared to look down from the mountain peaks on the hair-raising, stomach-churning ride. We swerved left and left again, careening around narrow bends so fast it seemed that we were about to fly into space and across the deep cavernous ridges. We ascended a fifty-degree slope, and when the sun began to rise behind the snow-capped mountains, I was aware only of the short distance between us and the oncoming car lights. The yellowish rays fell across the narrow turns. They seemed suspended from the top of the world.

Although we drove fast, Maurice was an experienced and cautious driver. Never very talkative, he hardly spoke a word during the long hours of the journey. I was not expecting any words to emerge from the stony profile beside me, so I was somewhat startled when I heard him say, "We're almost there, Mademoiselle."

I had been so exhilarated by the drive that I almost forgot my destination and the reason for it. At once, I collected myself and fumbled in my small bag for the letter, as the familiar sense of keen anticipation surged through me once more.

We were now on a flat road and out of the impressive mountain region. The streetlights were the first sign of civilization. We had driven all day and all night, and I felt quite tired and sleepy. My eyes were especially tired. I could still see the winding roads before me, although we had left them behind some while ago.

Maurice said nothing more until he slowed down to stop by a roadside. He checked the address, the number of the street; then, turning to me, he said, "Would you like me to come in with you, Mademoiselle?"

I was not quite sure what to say. I felt apprehensive and nervous.

"Or," he offered, "would you rather I wait here in the car until you make sure that they are at home?" He looked at his watch. "They should be up by now. It's nearly eight in the morning." He picked up the parcels while I waited outside the car. "Shall I take these in for you?"

"No, Maurice, thank you," I said, my knees feeling quite weak. "I'll be back for them, if they are home."

My hand trembled as I lifted the knocker fixed to the low wooden doorway and gave two distinct knocks with a weak shaky hand.

While I waited, I was certain that once the door opened, I would get a glimpse to my left of a certain banana tree. Shivering in the morning sunlight, I held the letter tightly, ready to hand it to my grandmother, as the door opened before me.

Chapter 58

Padlocking The Past

There, before my incredulous eyes, stood the woman with the hair tied in a bun at the back.

"Yes?" she said in an oddly superior manner. The voice sounded distant, yet familiar.

Before I replied, and shaking from head to foot, I craned my neck to the left because I wanted to verify that the house I had imagined was the real house. Sure enough, there stood the banana tree to my left, and there was the well, exactly where I knew it would be. It was an extraordinary feeling.

The woman stood waiting, staring at me with mildly curious eyes that reminded me of my mother's, but hers were veiled with suspicion. She left a small opening through which she poked her head. Curiosity had given way to a look of impatience, as one would look at a door-to-door salesman. I saw her glance across the street where Maurice sat waiting in the car.

"I am your granddaughter," I stammered, embarrassed by her rather cool attitude. "I've come all the way from Aleppo to bring you a letter from my mother." I tried to explain that my mother had dreamt of her and that she missed her and that she wanted me to meet her. The more I spoke, the less interested she looked. "That's Maurice, our driver," I added, pointing to the parked car and at the person at the wheel. "He drove me all the way here. Here's the letter my mother gave me to hand to you."

She took an abrupt step back, as if afraid of catching an infectious disease. I tried to clarify by repeating, "I am your granddaughter."

Her eyes widened as she put a hand over her mouth. Nothing could have prepared me for that reaction.

"Go away!" she ordered, looking terrified. "Go away and never come back!" She looked over her shoulder nervously as if afraid that someone would hear her, and she threw the unopened letter back at me.

"Go away, go before Johannes finds you here! We don't want anything to do with you! I don't want any letters from my daughter. Your mother disgraced us. Tell her to leave us alone!" She shut the door in my face.

I picked up the unopened letter and walked back to the car, but before I had a chance to tell Maurice about the cold reception I received, he said, "Get into the car, Mademoiselle, get into the car. I heard everything."

A terrible pain gripped my heart. I had merely touched the surface of my disturbing past without being allowed to explore it more fully. When the old woman shut the door in my face, she also shut me out of my childhood and padlocked the past so securely that I would never know where I was really born, or why I remembered the house in Iskenderun so well. And I knew I would never learn the truth from my own mother.

Chapter 59

Disowned

We reached home the following evening. When I told my mother that my grandmother had returned the letter to me without reading it, that she had refused to let me into her house, and that she had shut the door in my face, my mother commented sadly that at least we had tried and that there was nothing else that we could do.

My mother told me that while we were on our way to Iskenderun, she had attended Nevart's funeral. I, too, felt that I had attended a kind of funeral, but in Iskenderun, the demise of my childhood.

There were deep lines under my mother's eyes, and she seemed to have gained a bit of weight. I loved her so much! I did not know how to express it adequately. I snuggled up closer to her on the settee. We could hear the birds chirping outside. It was dawn. It was such a lovely day, but we seemed almost oblivious to it. She placed a protective arm around my shoulders, saying to herself somewhat absently that to forgive is supposed to be divine.

She never spoke again to me of her mother, but we did hear later from people who were aware of our failed trip to Iskenderun that my Uncle Johannes had sold the house, changed his name, and moved to another city in order to avoid any future unexpected visits from either of us. Whether or not that was true, it was the last news we ever had about my mother's real family. They had now disowned us completely, both emotionally and legally.

Chapter 60

Church On Sundays

In the gloom of this dark family situation, there shone a brief distraction in the form of Hubert, the shopkeeper and his family.

At first, Hubert was a companion, a straightforward and honest young man, as my mother would say, "Clean and decent." But one day, when he invited me to his home to meet his parents and sisters shortly before Christmas, sometime around 1944, I found out, for the first time in my life, what it was like to spend time with a closely knit family. I had never before, except in the movies, seen a father and a mother and children and cousins and uncles all together in the same house. That was a new experience, but not as unsettling as Hubert's behavior towards me the first time I found myself alone with him.

My mother at first made a few conventional objections to the visit; that is, to Hubert's plan to have a light supper at his place followed by a game of Monopoly and a few songs at the piano. But since the invitation came from Hubert's sister, Antoinette, who assured her that she would be with me the whole time, my mother could scarcely refuse. Not that she distrusted Hubert, mind you, but we all knew how people could gossip, and the fact was I was a single young woman being invited, without my mother, to a home by a man.

It promised to be a wonderful evening, and Antoinette turned out to be a lively and beautiful companion. She was quite unlike her brother except in the way she smiled. Her hair was cut short, in what, in those days, people called, "à la garçonne." She was a little older than Hubert; she had a few gray hairs, but these served only to accentuate her distinctive features.

I couldn't take my eyes off her, the way she sat and moved. And she was quick and intelligent; I was in awe of her, but not as completely overawed as I was at the beauty of their house.

We were in a room decorated with beautiful antiques, with two huge mirrors on opposite walls. The drapes were of heavy brocade with huge tassels elegantly holding them to either side, and the floor was covered with a thick oval carpet, in an attractive floral pattern in pastel shades on a bone-white background. At the opposite end of one wall, china figurines adorned the stands with Italian marble tops, and lights on a chandelier sparkled like an explosion of stars in the ceiling.

I met Hubert's mother, a tiny, bird-like lady with sparse white hair, who put down the book she was reading and peered up at me through half-moon spectacles, her thin, tight face smiling in a patch of fine wrinkles. She did not say much during supper. She ate with a sense of unhurried order, wiping her thin lips with meticulous precision. I was almost startled when she put a direct question to me about my school. The inquisition she put me through was brief but thorough. I managed to tell her some things about the American Missionary College for Girls.

Their house left a lasting impression on me. Not only for its layout and furniture, but more for the sense of security it afforded. My mother and I knew nothing of that feeling. Our house resembled a busy cage of rats. People dropped in and out, came and went. Nobody ever stayed. We felt nobody much cared what happened to us after the visitors left our house. In the end, my mother and I were always left alone.

I knew that the same kind of serenity reigned in Uncle's house. It was as if these two homes consisted of impregnable islands in the midst of rough, shifting seas. I knew also that

Fred's living room had a gold-plated ceiling. He had mentioned it to us on several occasions. That symbolized for me, at least, a sense of untarnished permanence, and made me marvel at the peace that such a home would engender. Hubert's family had lived together in the same house for years. They had no need to move or change or travel on concert circuits for months on end, while I slept all alone for years as a child and a young girl, as I had done at the orphanage. There seemed to be, for me, an unwelcome similarity somewhere.

I had felt somewhat uneasy at times during our meal because I felt Hubert's eyes constantly turning towards me, but I think he only meant to rescue me from his mother when he offered to give me a tour of the house, a mansion of beautiful passages, exercise rooms, and spacious bedrooms. He showed me the wine-cellar, which was not as large as the one at the Franciscan Convent on the other side of the Orphanage, but it seemed to hold a large assortment of bottles of quality red wines. Then, almost as an afterthought, Hubert led me into his own bedroom, where he showed off a brown and crumpled teddy bear sitting in a corner on the bookshelf above his bed.

Hubert, turning quite crimson for a moment, explained that his teddy bear had lost an eye during the war, when their house was slightly damaged when it was hit by a British bomb. "Rousseau, here, was the only casualty," he explained. "He fell out of the window and cracked his right eye." As I said nothing, Hubert went on, "We happened to be out at the time. I call him Rousseau because he is my father confessor."

I could not tell whether the tone in his voice was for me or for his teddy bear. I turned away to read some of the titles on his bookshelf, but he came round to my side and held the teddy bear out to me. "Would you like to have him?" He changed color again.

All I could think of saying was that we had to get back, but he went on in the most embarrassing way, telling me that

Rousseau would be glad to belong to me and sleep in my bed and share all my secrets. It made me feel uneasy, but he went on anyway.

"You may not realize this, but I believe Rousseau is in love with you."

That was more than enough for me. I walked out of his bedroom, and he followed me silently. We returned to the table. Hubert's mother, once again, began to take an interest in me. First, she commented on the excellence of my French. When I told her that I had learned the language at an orphanage, she expressed surprise.

"Oh, I didn't realize you were an orphan, you poor child!" she exclaimed.

Hubert tried to explain that away by telling his mother that my mother had also later sent me to the best convent school in the city.

"For one so young," Hubert's mother commented, "You seem to have attended many different schools in the city, my dear." All this time, the cousins and so forth were sitting comfortably in their armchairs, listening.

"Well, you see, Madame," I explained naively, "That's because I was expelled by so many."

Hubert's mother's expression grew cold, and I probably made things worse by explaining that my mother thought the nuns—not all of them, mind you, because there were some wonderful ones as well, but on the whole—were a bunch of narrow-minded old maids, who couldn't understand what went on outside their narrow world.

I saw her facial expression drop to a freezing point. "I presume your father is deceased since you say you were in an orphanage. Are you a Roman Catholic?" she enquired.

Hubert, who for some reason had decided to speak for me, gave a little speech about the differences between the Orthodox

Armenians and the Roman Catholics. All that seemed to me to be a long way off the point. I said nothing.

"I am told by my mother that I was born an Armenian Orthodox, but I was brought up by Roman Catholic nuns at the orphanage. But my mother is, what she calls herself, an agnostic. She believes in a universal or a spiritual, all-powerful force, she said. She says that all religions are good, provided they are not used as a weapon to hurt other people. People need to believe in something; we might feel lost without one, my mother says. But some people have their own, personal religion. She says, be good, help others, and try not to hurt anyone. That's what she believes."

Hubert's mother almost dropped the teacup. She wiped her lips again.

I babbled on, "I don't know my father's real name. My mother said that he had changed his name many times and was already married when he married my mother after changing his name again."

She was still staring at me with an open-mouth. I tried to smile but the look on her face stopped me short. I could not imagine what she might be thinking, but it seemed clear that I had offended her in some way simply by being honest.

"Do you and your mother attend church on Sundays?" she asked. I noticed Hubert's face turning red.

"My mother sends a carcass of cooked lamb every Christmas to be donated to the poor," I said proudly. "And she once told me that she likes small, empty churches, to be alone with God or whatever the great power might be, she says. She likes empty churches and small ones, Madame, and once she said that she prefers churches in villages, on a hilltop. I don't know why." I smiled feebly.

I felt trapped. Antoinette, Hubert, and the rest of his family sat listening to our conversation. It was as if they were watching a show. But Antoinette looked impatient, like she wanted to scold her mother for going on and on with her questions.

"Hubert was going to become a priest. Then, he changed his mind," his mother said, throwing a reproachful glance in his direction. He was still standing behind his settee, looking mesmerized.

"We attend church every Sunday. We haven't missed one yet. And we go with the family. There is comfort in a group, as well. But, if you never had a family, or you don't even know your own father, I can see how different things might be for your mother." She tried to be courteous, but I felt sorry I had accepted the invitation. There was no comparison between the noisy, musical atmosphere of our house with Hubert's posh, almost aristocratic, cool and courteous entourage. I could not imagine any member of his family using a word like "damn," for instance, without raising eyebrows.

When I got home later that day, my mother was at the theatre. I was glad of that. I did not want to go over the scene at Hubert's house. I preferred to let things go, to say nothing, and to keep the secret of the teddy bear offer to myself. Fortunately, my mother was not too curious about my visit to Hubert's house. The following afternoon, she asked, "How was it, darling?"

I responded simply by saying, "Oh, fine, they are very upright people, Maman."

"Good," she responded. And that was all.

Chapter 61

In The Breast Pocket

After one of my mother's performances, I was admitted into her dressing room, which was rather unusual, for she normally did not like to see anyone so soon after a performance, unless the person happened to be a dignitary of some sort. She was taking off her make-up, looking at herself in the mirror, when I walked in. I knew there was something wrong before I sat down.

She told me that she was tired of it all, that the new actor was an ass. She complained that his breath stank of alcohol, and that she hated going near him during the performance. "He doesn't even hear the prompter, for heavens' sake!" she moaned.

My mother rarely complained; she was usually stoic. That night, she looked tired. Even when she was finally ready to leave and seemed to have regained some of her old spirit, the deep lines under her eyes could not be hidden. I told her that she had only two more performances, two more nights, and that she could not walk out and let everybody down. I reminded her of how much the audience seemed to love and appreciate her talent. The standing ovations were remarkable, and that night, I had sat and marveled at its duration. For some reason, I felt I could talk to her with a mature voice now. "You are just tired, Maman," I reassured her.

"I know," she sighed, "but there are times I feel like throwing in the towel. You're right, darling. I must not. Not yet anyway. We must not give up." She said it as if trying to convince herself.

"Besides, we have to save enough money for your education. I must save, save, and save! It is sad that money is so important, but it is. I must milk Fred and everyone else as much as I can. By the way, I noticed that Fred is getting a bit reticent. Perhaps he is getting tired of me, who knows?"

Of course, my mother went right ahead and met her obligations by performing for the two remaining nights. But they took their toll. Her nerves suffered. And her kidneys were causing her excruciating pain. She looked pale and depressed. I compared her present shape with the old publicity pictures. Any pictures I was used to seeing at home and on the billboards on the streets showed her as a glamorous and beautiful actress. There was one, however, which hung in her bedroom that was unique. Ruba, her photographer and publicity agent—the man who had taken the photograph of me with Anush, years earlier—had taken a picture of my mother, dressed in one of her lavish stage costumes, very soft and lovely. I was there when that was happening, so I remember it quite well. He then dressed her in a man's suit, with a shirt and tie, and took the same picture again making it appear that there were two different people in the same picture. I was fascinated to see a young man staring flirtatiously at a young woman, realizing that they were one and the same person.

My mother started to lose interest in fashionable things. Also, she began to stay in her housecoat until late in the afternoon. She got rid of some of her poorer, less influential friends, appearing to be bored with men and with life in general, it seemed. The exuberance she had shown all these years beginning to diminish day by day.

We also confirmed that Fred was not paying his daily visits as regularly as before. And when he came, two or three times a week, he did not stay long. Another thing we noticed was that he no longer allowed my mother to go into his breast pocket to grab some money. He used to enjoy that in the past, but now it seemed to annoy him for some reason.

Chapter 62

The Young Girl

Hubert kept paying us regular visits, and, from time to time, he brought me some books and chocolate. My mother did not mind him inviting me to his house, and his family seemed hospitable and courteous, but I felt a little sensitive and uncomfortable in his mother's presence. She was always welcoming, albeit in a cool way. Antoinette continued to be warm, friendly, and jovial. I think she liked me.

When Hubert invited me to see an American movie during the matinée, my mother agreed I could go. The proviso was, "Don't stay out later than eight in the evening, Hubert. I trust you, but I don't trust people; they tend to gossip, especially with a young lady unaccompanied by her parents. You know all that."

Hubert was obliging and kept his word. But, by the oddest coincidence, while he and I were emerging from a local restaurant, I saw Fred sitting, having a drink with a young lady. I stopped for a minute and watched them, for I knew I could not be seen. I wondered who the person was. She looked a little older than me. I told myself she was likely a friend of the family because Fred had a huge family of many cousins and nieces. I felt sure that Fred was too fond of my mother to take out another woman. Something told me to keep the incident to myself. I might have been making a mountain out of a molehill.

Chapter 63

Au Revoir

As my mother decided to take it easy for a while and since it was summer time, she and I continued with our routine of taking a coffee at our usual place. And on one of those occasions, just as the waiter was serving us our dishes and the two coffees, I heard my mother whisper:

"Don't look now, but our cowboy friend is here…the one who addressed us out of the blue."

"The one who put his foot on one of our chairs and wanted to take me out for dinner, Maman?"

"Right, darling, that one."

We were barely half way through our coffee when, sure enough, the same Englishman made his way towards us. As my back was turned towards him, I had not seen him come.

"May I join you, ladies?" he enquired. He took out a handkerchief and wiped his forehead along the line his cap had made.

I tried to look surprised. "Oh, hello!" I said.

"May I?" he repeated pointing to the empty chair between my mother and me.

"What would you say if we said no?" my mother replied with a smile.

"I would try again," he responded.

"You never give up, do you?"

"Never," he replied grinning. "Well?" He held the back of the chair with one hand, his cap in the other, waiting.

"Sit down," said my mother with what little English she could still muster. She did not wish to attract people's attention. "What do you want from us, may I ask?" she added.

He sat down, thought it over for a minute, as if he did not know how to begin. When he did speak, he did so in a low voice, as if speaking confidentially, with great clarity, enunciating every syllable with care, "This will sound absurd, Madame, but I want to marry your daughter. If you allow me." Then he looked down at the cap he was holding on his knees.

My mother stiffened. Blood rushed to my head. I felt strangely embarrassed and shocked.

"You, sir," said my mother, with a touch of the dramatic gesture that I was so accustomed to seeing over the years, "are not funny. Please leave now."

But he was not easily put off. He smiled as he got up, staring at me with what I thought was with some genuine affection, and said: "Where have I heard this before?"

"Goodbye," my mother and I responded almost in a whisper, relieved to see him leave.

"Not goodbye, but au revoir," he added pushing his chair back in its place slowly, deliberately, and picking up his army cap. I did not wish to look back to watch him leave. My mother only spoke again when he had left the café.

"He will pester us each time we come to this place. What a weird thing to say, darling."

Chapter 64

The Porcupine & Marie

After the rape, we never rented a coach again. Instead, we took walks together along one of the avenues among other pedestrians and traffic, and we'd often stop for a sandwich, an ice cream, or a coffee. After that odd scene with the English soldier, my mother announced, "I'm going to take the car and we'll go tour the city as we used to do, darling."

My mother had learned to drive when she was young. The following day, she told Maurice that she was going to take the car. Then she asked three of her fellow actors and musicians to join us.

Everyone was laughing and joking when she drove by the same highway where she had been raped many years earlier. She slowed down a little as we approached the approximate spot where the coach had overturned.

She leaned over to whisper to me, as I was sitting next to her, while her friends were chatting and laughing in the back seats. "Remember, darling, these are hallowed grounds." I would never have recognized the unwelcome place had it not been for her. No one knew anything about it, of course, save for me and my mother.

In the car lights ahead, I saw a porcupine lumbering across the road. My mother put on the brakes and got out to catch it. To our astonishment, she ran back laughing like a child with a Christmas toy, holding the small prickly animal in her gloved hands.

"Look, everybody! They are nocturnal animals, like some of us. Look!" She held the creature by the open windows at the back of the car. One of her friends took the animal, and my mother returned to the wheel.

We returned home with the guests plus a porcupine. My mother wanted to keep it and look after it. After her friends left, she put the porcupine on the kitchen floor and closed the door behind her. She then got into her pajamas and housecoat. We sat together in the living room going over the day's events. My mother sat comfortably, but she did not look comfortable. She sighed and said, "Imagine finding a porcupine, darling. I have not driven a car for years and years. Just when I decide to get out anyway, we find a porcupine. It is a symbol of our lives, prickly as a porcupine. Vulnerable, and we like the dark. We come out at night." She always tried to look at the brighter side of things.

The porcupine disappeared the next day. It was as if we had imagined the whole thing. My mother could not believe it. She kept repeating, "But where could it possibly go?"

Even the next morning, when Marie arrived, my mother was up and still searching for the rodent. She explained to Marie what had happened, and every few minutes, my mother would shake her head incredulously and exclaim, "Where could it go?" Marie would respond, "I don't know, Madame."

Marie looked tired. She was doing too much work. She, too, was getting older. The porcupine was the least of her worries. For a few pounds a month, plus all the food and drink she and her children could consume or any incidentals, like a new dress or shoes, Marie worked from eight in the morning until about seven or eight o'clock at night, doing all the washing by hand, the ironing, darning, cleaning, cooking, and sometimes the shopping.

When I started having my periods, she washed all my sanitary napkins by hand, boiling them to sterilize them for reuse. She worked harder, now that Elias had left for Armenia. I am not sure how old Marie was, but she might have been in her sixties at the time. My mother gave Marie a few days off from time to time, but to me, it looked as if dear Marie should have retired altogether, which, of course, was out of the question.

During all the long years I had known Marie, I never heard her mention her husband. My mother might have known something about Marie's intimate life, but she never spoke about it, and yet Marie seemed, at times, closer to me than anyone else in the world. I can still see that kind expression on her lovely face. I can still distinguish her features. I can see wisps of hair, soaked in perspiration as she scrubbed our kitchen floor on her hands and knees. I often felt a strange sense of embarrassment to see such a fine woman on her knees washing our floors, perhaps in pain, while my mother and I sat chatting, eating, or entertaining guests.

Yet, Marie was fortunate to have my mother as the mistress of the house, not only because my mother sat and ate with Marie when they were alone, but she often insisted on serving Marie herself. Wearing Marie's apron, my mother would cook lamb chops for both Marie and me, over the open oven in our kitchen, which was something like an elevated fireplace in the wall, and order Marie to sit in at the head of the table while she served us both as she had often done when we were alone.

Marie was always touched by my mother's gesture of love and respect. She would cover her face with her grubby hands and bless Madame for being such an angel, while I would sit and look on, wanting so much to put my arms around the wonderful woman who had devoted so many years of her life to our service.

Chapter 65

Fred's Last Coffee

My mother found herself obliged to cut corners even further now, even going without make-up, now that Fred's visits were becoming less frequent. She appeared not to care whether he came or not; I had not mentioned the girl I had seen with him.

When he finally showed up at his usual time of around ten o'clock in the morning, my mother greeted him in her normal manner, as if he had never been away. She reached for the newspaper expecting another argument over politics, which, I have to say, was becoming somewhat tedious. Neither of us was prepared for the important news he was bursting to give us.

"I have some important news to announce," said Fred.

"The war is over?" My mother asked.

"No," he responded gravely, "I am engaged to be married."

My mother smiled and gave him a quick glance. "Oh, then it must be that charming young lady you've been taking out lately?"

My mouth fell open. I wasn't the only one shocked at my mother's words, as Fred registered open astonishment. "How did you know?" His face turned red.

"I have to know these things," my mother responded. She lowered her eyes again looking more interested in the news headlines. "After all," she added, "you and I have known each other for many years, Fred. We are friends. We have no secrets from each other."

Fred was nonplussed. My mother pretended to read, and then said, without turning her head from the paper, "Did she like her engagement ring?"

"Yes, she did."

My mother folded the paper resolutely. "So we shall not have the pleasure of your company any more, dear, dear Fred?"

"I wouldn't say that," he responded apologetically.

"What would you say then?"

As he fumbled for words, my mother continued speaking, unsmiling. "I heard your fiancée comes from a well-to-do family. Her dowry ought to be substantial. When is the happy day, may I ask?"

"In a few months' time."

"I hope you will find happiness."

Fred remained silent.

"Will you stay for a coffee or would that disturb your sense of fidelity?"

"I would like a coffee, thank you," he responded with unusual courtesy.

"It is Marie's day off," my mother explained, "I will go and make the coffee for us. I am afraid we seem to have fallen on hard times, lately."

I was not sure whether I should have retired to my room. I looked at her face. But she gave me no signal.

When the coffee was made, they sipped theirs noiselessly, an awkward signal of courtesy filling the gaps in their conversation. Finally, he slapped his knee with his manicured hand, "You make excellent coffee, my dear. Thank you." His tone was formal, as if we had just met. Then turning to me, he said, "Goodbye."

My mother opened the front door to let him out.

Something like pain gripped at my throat.

"I'd like to come and visit you from time to time, if I may?" he added somewhat lamely.

"Our house is always open to friends; we will be here, Fred. And all the best!"

As soon as the door was shut, my mother said, "We lost a gold mine, darling. Oh, what is to become of us? Now where am I going to get the money to buy you your bracelet of independence? Your future, darling?"

I could not help but wonder how my mother knew about Fred's engagement, but I remembered her large circle of acquaintances, among them, Karnik, the jeweler and his business colleagues. And the movements of the elite of the city seemed to be of interest to most of the population.

It was hard to believe that Fred was getting married. I did not particularly miss him, for I never cared for him much, but I felt sorry for my mother who seemed even more depressed now that she could no longer play her pseudo-political part with him, as a preliminary to taking him for all the money he could afford.

Chapter 66

A Second Marriage Proposal

Fred may have left us, but Hubert kept up his visits. I went out with him from time to time, provided that I was back home at the time specified by my mother. He was allowed to take me to the movies as long as I was home by nine-thirty.

One afternoon, Hubert arrived while my mother and Marie were busy in the kitchen. He waited for her to come into the living room. He had a special message for her.

When my mother entered the living room, after the usual warm greetings, my mother asked Hubert to make himself comfortable. As soon as he was seated, he looked straight at my mother. Without mincing words, he said, "Madame, I would like to marry your daughter. But because I have objections from certain members of my family, I am considering moving to South America where I have other relatives, who are doing well in the export business. I can join them if I so choose. But I would have to sell my boutique here and leave and then send for your daughter. All this is contingent upon your acceptance of my offer to marry your daughter, Madame."

Both my mother and I were nonplussed. I never expected two successive marriage proposals within such a short time. I was curious to see what my mother would say. Hubert was a fine fellow, but I considered him a comrade, nothing more. He was fun to be with, to listen to.

"My daughter is too young to get married, Hubert. This is

no reflection on your character. She is too young. And, to be frank with you, she must get a university degree of some sort. She has a few more years to go."

"I can wait," he responded. "There is no hurry, Madame."

"Is it all right with you?" my mother asked.

"Of course," agreed Hubert.

Chapter 67

The Last Summer

Summertime meant that our house was filled with the aroma of tomatoes, oranges, and grapefruit from the ports of Haifa and Jaffa. During those hot, stifling July days, I would sit and watch my mother and Marie at work in the kitchen.

Sacks filled with fruit and vegetables and nuts of all kinds spilled over the kitchen floor. Oranges were squeezed and boiled, their juices poured into sterilized jars or glass bottles to be served later during the season, always diluted with water, or ice.

Tomatoes covered the whole surface, to be peeled and boiled and salted lightly and poured into shallow, wide pans, then left on the rooftop to dehydrate to a thick, rich paste. I would often go to the rooftop to watch Marie or my mother stir the paste every morning and evening, regularly at sunrise and sunset, carrying the pans down to the kitchen at the end of the day…until the next day, when they took them back up to the rooftop to dry under the hot July sun.

Every evening, I would sit on the hot cement floor of our roof, sometimes staying there for hours, watching the stars and listening to the sound of the wonderful concert the dry eggplants made. Being hollow and light, they were often caught by the summer evening breeze and tossed about gently, making them knock together like bongo drums. I would sit and listen, enchanted by the sounds made by these huge mauve vegetables, which overnight had become transformed into veritable instruments of music.

I have a vague memory of watching my mother and Marie prepare another treat, but I cannot remember the name of it. The process involved covering huge bed sheets with some jelly-like substance, which also dried in the sun and which was later gently peeled off, like a band-aid, filled with nuts, and cut into so many five- to ten-inch-long segments to be consumed later. They reminded me of jellybeans, except that these were much longer and some had a string running through their middle. I know they tasted delicious, and I have never seen anything like them in all my travels. I shall always remember seeing those clean white sheets hanging heavily on clotheslines, along with the marvelous eggplants. Those summer evenings, during school vacation, were among the happiest moments of my early life.

As the months passed, I grew taller than my mother. She was a little over five feet; I now passed her by nearly five inches.

Chapter 68

Old Regime's Disguise

One day, as I stood alone before the full-length mirror, studying my own reflection with a more critical eye, I was suddenly taken back to the memory of the reflection of a skinny, ill-clad child I used to be, with dark complexion and huge sad eyes.

Now, I stood taller than my mother, I was much better clad, a little less skinny with budding breasts…but there was still the same kind of strangely frightened look in my eyes. Yet, something seemed to have altered in me almost overnight.

My eyes traveled with deliberate slowness from the soles of my white sandals to the top of my jet-black hair, until I was staring into my own eyes, which seemed huge, yearning for an answer to a question I could not even put into words. The expression on my face was lackluster— sad, hurt, and questioning. I likened myself as a petrified bird caught in flight and chained by its ankles.

I had no idea why I felt as I did. There, staring back at me, was the sad young face of someone who did not know where she came from and, perhaps more importantly, where she was going in life. Something was pressing me on into a future I could not imagine, and I was hanging in limbo, searching into my soul. Just then, the reflection of a young woman in a black costume with a red rose on her lapel came into view over my shoulder.

"The face of the war is altering, Ano," my mother said, using the nickname she sometimes called me.

As I did not quite understand, she went on to explain that the January 1943 planned meeting in Casablanca, with Roosevelt, Churchill, and Stalin (which Stalin ultimately did not attend) would seal Germany's fate.

"It can't take too long now," she sighed, as if she was talking to herself.

I caught sight of the newspaper in her hand. I thought briefly of Fred, whom we had not seen for quite some time.

My mother seemed to have noticed, with mild disapproval, that, for some reason, I was beginning to take more interest in my appearance than in war news. She sighed again and spoke of the war on the Russian front and the counter offensive of Stalingrad, of the Axis troops surrendering by the thousands, of Marshal Timoshenko in the Ukraine. Her face was pale. She looked tired. When she saw that I did not know how to respond to her news, she went to the settee and began to read the second newspaper. Marie had left it there for her.

Chapter 69

Allied Forces Attack

During one of his visits to our house, Uncle opened an Arabic newspaper and said, "There is something here about Lord Haw-Haw. You know, he used to broadcast to us from Berlin. Apparently, he was not a German at all, but a naturalized German. It says here his real name was William Joyce of New York City, but he lived in England and lied about his origins. Very interesting, don't you agree?"

My mother could not read Arabic, so she simply listened. Uncle spoke from behind the newspaper. "I see that the Allied forces are attacking German cities now. It is the reverse of the German Blitzkrieg. According to this, the Allies are bombarding Hamburg as they did Cologne. It looks bad for the Germans. The tide is turning. Hitler's glory years from 1939 to 1942 seem to be almost over. Now, we are in 1944, and it looks as though the end cannot be far. Of course, America helped a great deal, and Russia is not an enemy to be tampered with. America is rich. It helped Britain in its darkest hour. Hitler could not have imagined it. Who could have? The Americans went all that distance to help Britain. There we are. Anyway, I brought you some Armenian newspapers to read."

Uncle did not look as sad as when he had first arrived that day. It was always a pleasure to listen to Uncle, for he was rarely rash in his statements. Unlike Fred, he made no grandiose gestures when he spoke. He displayed no undue emotionalism when discussing any subject. The whole house was filled with a sense of peace when he was present. Suddenly, he looked at me and smiled, "You sit and listen and wonder," he said to me. "Whatever happens, the war cannot last too long now, from what we read in the newspapers and hear on the radio. You will be able to obtain your law degree, Inshallah!"

Chapter 70

A Real Name

In July 1944, the newspaper headlines announced Erwin Rommel's suicide by poisoning. It shocked many people, including some of the British soldiers.

The concentration camps and all the details made their public appearance after 1944. People were incredulous. They could not believe that these things could take place. The public social attitude began to alter, at first, almost imperceptibly. For example, in the past, people rarely spoke to strangers in cafés, no matter how overcrowded the places were. But now, people fell into conversation in the most matter-of-fact way. It was as if the end of the war had brought serenity and friendship to the locals.

At one of the cafés, my mother and I met an American geologist who worked for the British-American Oil Company. After his third beer, he asked my mother if he could take me to Caracas, Venezuela, with him as his secretary. I caught my mother's eye and laughed. Hubert had also wanted to take me to South America.

Around us, people chatted loudly and laughed. British soldiers and officers sat with civilian families at various tables. There was a relaxed atmosphere about the whole place, which had become the center of the chic and the elite of the city.

The geologist's face looked as tough as leather. His eyes were deep and blue. His hair was a dirty blond and thinning on top. He was tall, lean, and wiry looking. He had the complexion and the physique of an outdoors man. He gulped down his beer and ordered another. From the way he poured the drink and held the bottle and mug, it was easy to tell that he had many years of practice at it, as his somewhat crimson complexion could testify.

He seemed to be a mellow person. His friendly, decent smile traveled our faces one by one, with open pleasure. His voice and dialect fascinated me. It was fun listening to his deep cowboy drawl. As the level of beer went down in his mug, the rate of his eagerness to take me with him seemed to grow.

My mother humored him by saying that poets made poor secretaries. But he kept repeating his offer until a few weeks later the day came when he had to leave without me.

Some weeks after the geologist's departure, a face we had almost forgotten re-emerged out of this congenial crowd of people at the same café. It was the uniformed Englishman. He stood, staring down at us, and repeated his familiar, "May I join you?" request.

He was speaking to my mother, but he kept his eyes on me. "It's been a long time," he added.

My mother told him she hoped he had been posted somewhere by now. He did not appear to be annoyed with her.

"I will be leaving shortly. The war is over. May I?" he repeated courteously.

My mother nodded.

He sat down looking as if amused at some private joke. He offered us a drink, but my mother declined. After a long silence, during which he drank his coffee, my mother asked him what part of England he came from.

"London," he replied.

"What kind of work did you do before?" she asked. It was obvious that she meant before the war.

"I was a tailor," he replied and he kept looking at me with an odd sort of tenderness that bothered me.

My mother then asked him if he was a good tailor, only half in jest. He said, "Do you mean, Madame, was I a good man who made suits for a living, or a man who was good at his trade, or a good man who was also a good tailor?"

That made everybody laugh. Abraham seemed more like a philosopher than a tailor. And I said so.

"Why not?" he asked merrily, "I am a soldier and a tailor. I could also be a philosopher, a soldier, and a tailor or, on the other hand, I could be bad at all three."

In the midst of the laughter that followed, he told us that he still wanted to ask the same old question. He lit a cigarette and took a deep puff as he glanced at the strollers walking arm in arm. They floated around like milkweed seeds released into the open air, carried here and there by the lovely evening breeze. There was a strangely dream-like quality to the whole scene.

"May I marry your daughter, Madame?" he asked looking straight at my mother and then intently at me.

"Are you divorced?" countered my mother.

"As a matter of fact, Madame, I have never been married. There was a girl once, years ago, but she has since married an American she met in London."

My mother's expression suddenly altered; she looked serious. She frowned. I, too, felt nervous for some reason, but tried not to show it.

"I wanted my daughter to attend university," my mother said, "that was the dream I always had for her, now that the war is over. But I realize it will be expensive. I could, perhaps, manage the first year or two but it is going to prove to be difficult to manage the whole fee."

Abraham said, "Why don't you send her to England, instead? There, I could help her with some or the rest of her university fees. I was a good tailor. I was financially quite comfortable. I can do it. Trust me, Madame. I will promise to send your daughter to the university, but in England, and I will help her until she obtains her degree in whatever field she chooses. I will undertake to send your daughter to school. There is a good university in London, Madame. I, myself, have spent many an evening in their library, poring over books."

He looked convincing. Even my mother seemed impressed.

"Evenings?" asked my mother with interest.

"Yes, because I had to work during the day while I became a tailor and earned a good living. But I wanted to get a degree in literature. I love reading."

The end result of this meeting was that Abraham was invited to our house for lunch the next day.

After lunch, my mother explained that our cook, Elias, had left for the Soviet Union, as thousands of Armenians had done.

Abraham commented that people who have been persecuted need a homeland.

My mother told him that the whole globe ought to be our homeland. "This is what causes wars in the first place," she added, "thinking that a certain geographical location is reserved for a certain ethnic, religious, or racial group. No one owns the soil on which we live. In fact, it owns us. When we look back at history, we see so many changes and we have to accept them. Even the names of countries change over the centuries."

"Yet," said Abraham, with a deep sigh, "every human being wants peace. This is such a contradiction to what has been taking place over the centuries. But who knows what the future holds. Thank heavens the war is over, Madame."

We'd retired to the living room, and now Abraham sat in the armchair, with my mother sitting in another one, facing him. He took a sip of his coffee and cleared his throat. "I fell in love with your daughter, Madame, as soon as I set eyes on her for the first time. I would like to marry her. I would like to take her back to England with me. I promise to look after her, and to send her to school. I give you my word, Madame."

I felt somewhat embarrassed to be standing, listening to the conversation while my mother and this stranger decided my own future for me. But I hardly had any choice or reason to reject the offer; the timing was right and the opportunity to go to university might not come again. At least Abraham looked like an honest person, even if he did smoke too much.

After Abraham left, my mother half smiled, raising her shoulders as if she, herself, was not yet sure. "Perhaps we have no better choice. Maybe providence sent him to us. Who knows? I'll have to sleep on it."

I did not quite know what to think. That night, I lay in bed, wondering how a complete stranger could suddenly become so important in our lives, opening a door through which I could realize some of my dreams. I would leave behind all the ugly memories of the orphanage, of my mother's rape, of Herunt, when he had beaten up that poor young man, and the shame and humiliation I had lived with all my life. I could shake off the curse of my birth as an illegitimate, nameless girl. It would all be eradicated. I would become an English citizen, go to school, study and write, or become a lawyer and write. I would be independent, in a sense. I would be able to work; with both of us working, we would have a comfortable life and send for my mother someday. I would live like the girls in the Hollywood, French, or English movies and have a home and decent neighbors. Above all, I would have a real name.

It seemed promising, yet the following day, when my mother wanted to know if I felt anything for the British soldier, I started to weep. My mother tried to reassure me that there was no hurry whatsoever, that within a few days we would take a holiday together, just the two of us, and come back with the best possible solution, even though it might mean a period of separation.

Chapter 71

London Calling

Time was running against us; Abraham was at our doorstep in no time. He explained that he had to return to civilian life soon after his return to England.

I was paralyzed with indecision. I could not sit there, in the living room, facing Abraham and say nothing.

My mother asked me, once again, whether I felt any kind of warmth at all for Abraham.

I blushed and stammered, "I don't hate him, Maman."

When Abraham reappeared at our door the following day and sat down beside my mother, waiting for her to say something, my mother said, "My daughter is not in love with you, Abraham. She is young and innocent."

He was not in the least put out. "She will love me when she gets to know me better. I know she is innocent. And you said that she has only recently become fully pubescent, Madame. I am thirty-three years old. I will know how to take care of her, I assure you."

It is true that I had only just begun to menstruate that year. I felt as if a demon had invaded my body. I saw it as a filthy instrument of evil. Nevertheless, there really was little to discuss about the marriage proposal. The choice was obvious. I would have to marry Abraham; my mother agreed.

Abraham took my mother's hand and kissed it. He told us both how pleased he was. He once again promised to take good care of me and to send me to school as soon as we settled down in England. He said we would never regret the decision, not for a moment. It was touching to see him look so delighted.

My young heart was oversaturated with a kind of romantic indifference. I looked at Abraham as a cow might stare at a pond. He was there. And I was here. I felt no stirrings of real warmth, passion, or deep affection. I was at a loss as to what it would be like to be this stranger's wife, to live with him for the rest of my life in a place far away called London.

I, who had never left home except to attend various schools, could not visualize my own person somewhere far away from my dearest Maman, the only person I had loved in the whole world. To leave her and to go with a stranger, to cross the oceans, to settle somewhere, seemed intimidating to say the least. Yet, the future without this prospect looked even dimmer.

Abraham told us that he would leave immediately to obtain our marriage permission, which would take from two weeks to a month, but that he would try to rush it through since research into my background would be simpler now that the war was over. He told my mother that it would be a simple military wedding.

He could not leave soon enough. Like an unwanted genie, he disappeared in his jeep in a great big cloud of dust. My mother, Marie, and I stood at the front door watching the road, immobile and wonderstruck.

Chapter 72

A Visitor At My Own Wedding

Our marriage consisted of a simple registration process. Our papers were in good order; it took less than half an hour. We returned to the city to celebrate at one of the rented banquet balls, not far from Hubert's boutique. (Hubert went on with his business as though he had never proposed to me; my mother had made it quite clear that running away to get married in South America was not a good idea.)

For the occasion, I wore a magnificent dress specially designed and made by Charlotte. It was left on display for about a week in one of the famous shop-windows of the city for passersby to admire. It was made of blue taffeta with handmade violets, each of which took hours for her to design and cut, and my mother wanted each flower to be a little different from the other, "As in nature," my mother had told Charlotte. My slip and brassiere, as well as my panties, were all made by hand in matching silks.

My mother offered to pay for the catering, the photographers, the two different bands, and other incidentals. The first band played for those who stayed till midnight, and the second one followed to accommodate those who enjoyed themselves till dawn.

Abraham invited some dignitaries, and so did my mother. Her steadfast photographer friend Ruba took pictures to catch every mood, every pose from every conceivable angle, of every person present.

The eight-tiered wedding cake was a masterpiece of design. The tablecloths were strewn with fresh roses of all hues. The food was worthy of the occasion. The crystal chandeliers glittered over the bright marble floors of the banquet hall.

I danced with some of the guests, but I felt more like a visitor to my own wedding celebration than an integral part of it. I felt unexcited to the point of emotional numbness. Abraham, on the other hand, looked ecstatic. He was laughing and joking and being congratulated by everyone. He smoked one cigarette after another. The ashtrays were full of his cigarette butts. The waiters kept emptying them as fast as he tried to fill them.

We danced together under admiring eyes; while in his arms, I thought back to a movie I had been to with my mother as a young girl, after I had left the orphanage. A beautiful couple danced at their wedding looking radiantly happy. I wondered why I could not feel the same flow in myself. I moved mechanically, floating lightly on my toes on the slippery dance floors, as in a vast palace of strangers.

While we were dancing, an unpleasant odor wafted by. For a second, I wondered where it came from. But we kept on dancing. Abraham did not understand why I was so silent. "You are not exactly a chatterbox, are you?" he teased. I remember that sentence well because I had never heard the word chatterbox before. I asked him what it meant, and he told me. He also taught me another word that night and that was the word halitosis, which he explained meant bad breath.

Just then, I saw my mother walking towards us. She looked beautiful but not exactly happy. She made every effort to appear cheerful. She told us that Uncle had dropped by for a few minutes to congratulate us. We followed her through a sea of smiling faces and hands holding champagne glasses and bracelets encrusted with bright jewels that, now and then, caught the lights, sending broken rainbows everywhere.

Uncle stood away from the crowd by the entrance—small, brown, and silent, almost sad, I thought. He smiled upon seeing us and took a few steps towards us. He held his fez in one hand. When he took my hand with the other, I did something I had never dared do during all the years I had known him. I threw myself into his arms and cried.

Taken by surprise, Uncle stood beside Abraham and my mother somewhat awkwardly. He took me aside and said, "Congratulations to you both. And I must say you look charming." That was all. My mother could not convince Uncle to stay. She walked him to the exit.

As far as I was concerned, the wedding celebrations did not suggest a sense of security. Rather, they aroused in me some trepidation and brought back the day my mother had come to the orphanage to visit me, where my sense of imprisonment overrode any eager anticipation. I felt the same kind of entrapment now, the nature of which I was not yet able to decipher or define. A door had opened, but who was to know what, exactly, lay on the other side of it?

Chapter 73

Tides Of Fate

After the wedding ceremony, Abraham and I began to get ready for the trip to England, after a brief honeymoon at a seaside resort.

Things were changing quickly, and I think I was in a mild state of shock. Here I was being driven to a new destination. It was a bit like the time my mother had come and claimed me back from the orphanage after so many years. I had sat beside her, in the back of her car, wondering where life was taking me. Now, I sat beside my husband quietly, letting the tides of fate blow me in any direction it decided. I was not able to make small talk. I barely had time to get over the incredible events at my wedding celebration and the honeymoon. I had never danced with a man before, I had never been surrounded by so many admiring eyes before; I had never been the center of attention before—at least, not in this way. The only occasion when I was the centre of attention was when I had to carry the sign saying, "Je suis une fille désobéissante." Even then, the orphans did not care what sign anyone carried.

All too soon the day of separation rushed at me like a death sentence. I had to say goodbye to my mother. I wept and dabbed my soaking cheeks. She, too, sobbed. Marie stood unobtrusively at a short distance. Her wrinkled face was full of pain. My mother took me in her arms for the last time. During our goodbye, Abraham waited in the jeep. The afternoon August sun was hot; the engine was running.

"Be strong, darling," my mother whispered. "Be strong. We have no other choice. This is the only way out. Make sure you get your Golden Bracelet of Independence, darling. You must attend university in England. I am sure your husband will keep his word. And if he doesn't, then at least we'll know within about a year, and, what's a year in a life, darling? You're young. I have enough money saved now to send you to a university for at least a year. In the meantime, I'll do my best to add to those savings. Go now. I must say he looks like an honest man. Go, darling. Go! He is waiting!"

I sat beside Abraham. The jeep started to move. Through the open car window, I heard my mother cry out in a voice of utter despair, "Write to me! Write to me, darling! Don't forget to write to me!"

I never saw my mother again.

Epilogue

Written by Antonia Swann

My mother chose to end this account with her moving away, as it captured the most intense time in her relationship with Hosanna, but their story was far from finished. My mother led quite the extraordinary life, and I believe I have her blessing to share with you how it all turned out. While these are my words, this is very much Anahid's story.

Anahid moved to Leicester, England with Abraham, to live with his mother, while Hosanna stayed in Aleppo, Syria. Once they settled, Anahid wrote to her mother regularly, but she soon began to worry because she never received any letters from Hosanna.

One day, months later, Anahid discovered a stack of letters, all wrapped up tightly with a red string, at the bottom of the front hall closet. All of them were from Hosanna. Anahid sat there on the floor of the front hall for hours, opening them, one after another. As the letters progressed, her mother's tone became more and more desperate and Anahid learnt that her mother's health was declining.

With the pile of letters in hand, my mother first asked Abraham about it. He said he had no idea. Anahid then confronted

Abraham's mother, who simply shrugged her shoulders and walked away, muttering that Anahid did not deserve to have a mother as she had taken away her son. Anahid and Abraham separated just over a year later.

Anahid then moved to London in order to pursue her dream of obtaining her "Golden Bracelet of Independence". She immediately wrote to Hosanna explaining the situation, and mother and daughter resumed regular contact. Both were relieved to be back in touch. Hosanna contacted people in the UK to help arrange a divorce and find my mother a place to live.

My mother got her first job: selling stockings on the main floor of Selfridges, a huge department store in central London. Because she had been quite sheltered by Hosanna, she thought buses only went between cities, and because of this, she took a taxi to and from work, every day. When her boss asked her why she came to work every day by taxi, my mother responded, "Because I don't own my own car, ma'am." Shortly after that (and with her boss's help), my mother moved into a girls' residence on Wigmore Street, directly behind Selfridges; she no longer had to take taxis.

Selfridges held an annual beauty contest that attracted thousands of girls. My mother's friend put Anahid's name in for it and Anahid became Miss Selfridge. She was awarded first prize by a famous movie star of the time, Bill Owen. I have photos of them smiling for the cameras. My mother actually bought a small dog to go with her silver-fox jacket for that occasion.

After working at Selfridges for several months, my mother got promoted to an office job as an administrative assistant. Her boss became a good friend. One day, while walking out of a laundromat with her boss, my mother met my father, Anthony (Tony) William Swann, who happened to be her boss' brother-in-law.

She always told me how calm she thought my father's blue eyes were when she first saw him. He was apparently very elegant, with his beret, pipe, and walking stick. My father matched the definition of an "Englishman" that Hosanna had implanted in Anahid's mind years earlier.

Tony became the love of Anahid's life and about two years later, in 1954, they married in London. Hosanna was not happy to find out that my mother was marrying another Englishman and did not attend the wedding. Still, Hosanna and Anahid continued to write.

Several years later, Hosanna wrote to Anahid to ask her to find a specialized medicine for a friend. My mother searched everywhere but could not find it. Hosanna was not pleased at this news and wrote to express her anger and disappointment in Anahid. Anahid apologized, but Hosanna was very hurt and stopped writing. My mother wrote many letters to Hosanna trying to explain. Eventually, Anahid just gave up, but she never stopped hoping for another letter.

In 1956, my parents emigrated to Canada on the RMS Ivernia ocean liner, to start a new life. They settled in Toronto, Ontario, where my mother wrote syndicated columns and book reviews for *The Toronto Telegram.* During this time, she was published in *Mayfair Magazine*, *Delta Magazine* and *The Canadian Forum.* Along the way, she garnered several writing awards, including one from the Canadian Author's Association.

She also did book reviews on CFTO-TV in Toronto for six years, developed a segment called "Better Late" with Wessely Hicks for the CBC and had scripts produced by CFTO-TV.

Anahid appeared on various television shows including "Front Page Challenge", and "The Pierre Berton Show". It was at this time that Anahid and Pierre Berton became lifelong friends, moving in the same circles, meeting at various parties and events, and exchanging letters. I still have several of his letters to my mother.

Whenever she could, Anahid began penning her memoir,

drawing on some of her earliest memories in life. Pierre believed in her memoir, calling it "undeniably interesting" in one of his letters. He would later visit my mother's schools to give talks when she began teaching.

After my father's promotion, in 1966, my parents moved from Ontario to Manitoba. My mother was now finally in a position to pursue her dream of higher education full-time.

In Winnipeg, she obtained her double honours in English and French Literature. Anahid then also received her Bachelor's in Education followed by a Master of Arts in English Literature, her Master's thesis specializing in James Joyce's Ulysses – one of the most challenging subject areas possible.

It was during this period that she shortened her first name and became known as "Ann Swann". From the early 1970s, my mother became a beloved teacher of French and English to thousands of students, both in Fort Rouge and Fort Gary, in Winnipeg, Manitoba, and later in Aurora and Newmarket, Ontario. During her teaching career, my mother was interviewed by a local newspaper. In the article entitled "Meet A Teacher Who is Not Average", she was described as a "French teacher at Regency Acres Public School [who] has led the type of life most of us have only experienced through books, and might not be able to cope with if we were forced to follow in her footsteps."[1]

In 1978, my father died suddenly, of cancer. He had made dinner for us the night before, when my mother was in night school, at the University of Winnipeg. Throughout all this, my mother still wrote to Hosanna.

A year later, a final letter came from Aleppo. It was sent from Hosanna's neighbors. I recall my mother opening the letter with great trepidation. I was seventeen years old. The letter shared the news that Hosanna had passed away. Her neighbors added that Uncle never left her side—he stayed with Hosanna to the end.

---

[1] The Aurora-King Banner, July 8, 1981, written by Dan O'Reilly

I remember my mother read the letter stoically, then quietly passed it to me. I read it and gave it back to her and put my arms around her. She folded it in two and walked upstairs calmly to file it away in her blue filing cabinet in her study. She never talked about that letter ever again.

Since the mother-daughter relationship between Anahid and Hosanna shaped much of who my mother was, I also want to share a little of the mother-daughter relationship Anahid and I had. Like Hosanna, my mother was protective, practical, and quirky.

She took me to Shoppers Drug Mart when I was nineteen years old to buy condoms and all things "reproductive," when I was just starting to date my late husband. I have images of the condom boxes and other special reproductive items (including a douche and fancy female freshener), moving painfully slow along the Shoppers check-out conveyor belt. At the very end of the conveyor belt, trailing all the regular family planning items, was a small bottle of Lysol.

As the items were bagged, my mother noticed an odd expression on the cashier's face. My mother, unabashed, explained that a few drops of Lysol were "absolutely necessary for women for the special cleaning afterword," to which the cashier responded, "Isn't Lysol for the floors, Ma'am?" I couldn't get out of Shoppers fast enough.

Her protective nature would end up being more than a funny anecdote, though we didn't know it at the time. It was because of her very pro-condom stance that that I never got HIV/Hepatitis C-tainted blood years later, when my late husband, James Kreppner, contracted both of these diseases during Canada's tainted blood scandal (James became one of a handful of activists to secure the largest class-action settlement in Canadian history for thousands of Canadians). My mother's strong belief and advice to me to always insist on condoms lowered my risk of acquiring these two deadly infections and possibly saved my life. To this day, I am grateful for that.

Throughout the decades my husband lived with HIV and Hepatitis C, my mother became like a second mom to him, ensuring he ate regularly (especially when he had no appetite) and took his pills. Most importantly, she helped me through those rough years. I was his primary caregiver, and my mother constantly made sure I, too, was being looked after.

I have a photograph of my mother with my husband, at Finch Station in Toronto, taken in the late 1990's. In this photo, my mom has her arm tightly around him, and both are looking right at the camera. When he was healthy, my husband (who was 6 feet tall) weighed 180 lbs. At a mere 88 lbs, this image captured him looking extremely gaunt. I can see strength and sadness in my mother's eyes knowing that he would probably die before her.

Even in her later years, my mother never stopped missing her own mother. Sometimes, before she fell ill, she would hear a bird sing at twilight on one of our regular mother-daughter evening walks and remind me that its call sounded like "Ano," the nickname Hosanna had given her. She would pause and be sad every time. Just for a moment. Then we would keep walking.

Over the years, her once jet-black wiry hair became soft and almost pure white, but her eyebrows were still quite dark. Months before, when she was still independent enough to be at home, I would do her hair, using twist ties from bread bags to secure the tiny pig tails I'd fashioned. She looked very cute—like some kind of moon animal. I remember her with all the white twist ties I had put in her hair, smiling like a child, sitting at her kitchen table at home.

Thirteen months after my husband died, my mother had a series of heart attacks. She became weaker and weaker and less and less aware. In her last weeks, she was admitted to a local community hospital, north of Toronto.

She was drifting in and out of consciousness for several days and I had been at the hospital about an hour one day when she woke up, suddenly, and looked at me, her eyes clear and bright.

"Mom?" she asked innocently.

"No, I'm the daughter and you're the mother," I said.

She smiled at me, reassured, closed her eyes, and drifted back to sleep.

On what was to be her last night, I got up to give her a kiss goodnight before heading home for dinner. I don't know why, but before leaving her hospital room, I whispered in her ear, "Don't worry mom, I will do something with the book. See you tomorrow. Sleep well." There was no reaction; she continued sleeping.

I left to have a late dinner just before visiting hours ended. After dinner, my gut said to go back to the hospital to check in even though I knew visiting hours were over. It was just a ten-minute drive away.

On my way back to her room, I walked by her nursing station. A nurse told me she was very sorry about my mother, which confused me because I had not received their urgent message, as I was in transit when they phoned.

Shocked, I ran down the hospital corridor to her room. Her body was there but my mother was gone.

I don't know why, but I stayed by her bedside for seven hours alone till about four in the morning, after a priest had come to do last rites. Apparently, my mother had requested a Catholic priest some days earlier.

As I noted in the Foreword, I knew Anahid's greatest wish was to have her memoir published. While reviewing and editing my mother's memoir, to prepare it for publication, each time I got closer to the end of the memoir, I would start to feel sad. This is because I knew the end of the book was coming. However, each time I reread it, I would feel reconnected to her, which is a true gift.

My grandmother's sacrifices allowed my mother to flourish and, ultimately, become a completely self-sufficient teacher in the West, after obtaining multiple advanced degrees. Anahid was awarded the Gold Medal in French Literature by the University of Winnipeg for her work specializing in Molière, the knowledge of which was drawn from her childhood experiences watching her mother, Hosanna, on the stage all those years ago. This stream of academic accomplishments followed a rich set of writing experiences, including awards for her stories and poetry and productions of her screenplays.

My mother was my best friend, which is something she used to say about her mother. She also sacrificed a lot for me and my brother, as her mother did for her— always putting our needs before hers. My brother and I grew up knowing our mother was unlike other mothers.

Anahid helped and encouraged me and my brother to pursue higher education, me with my Ph.D. in economics and my late brother, Peter Swann, with his degrees in music production, composition and theory, allowing him to thrive in music. Our mother was so happy when my brother won First Place in Toronto's Fender Guitar Warz Contest. She'd tell everyone that Pete taught guitar to Alex Lifeson's son (of Rush fame). Just one year before she passed away, she came with me to my York University Ph.D. graduation, proudly smiling and taking photos. The success my brother and I achieved in life was only made possible by the extraordinary lineage of women who came before us.

Even though it has been many years since she passed, I still feel my mother's powerful spirit, just as she often told me that she regularly felt her own mother's presence well after she had died. Both were extraordinary women and mothers, who loved and protected each other above all else. Hosanna's dedication to her daughter allowed not only Anahid to gain freedom through education, but also allowed me and my brother, in turn, to achieve own "Golden Bracelets of Independence," ensuring we had the best tools to survive.

Hosanna would have been proud. E!

Anahid Hagopian in Toronto at one of the first places she and her husband, Tony lived. Not long after Ann and Tony emigrated to Canada, they settled in Toronto. August, 1957.

Anahid with Pierre Berton (left) and Janet Berton (right) at her 1992 retirement party in Newmarket, Ontario.

Antonia (Smudge) Swann (left), Anahid and Peter Swann (right) bowling for Anahid's birthday in Aurora, Ontario. Mid 1990's.

Anahid (Ann Swann) writing at her writing desk in Winnipeg marking students' exams. The Swanns moved from Toronto to Winnipeg after Tony got promoted by the Canadian Manufacturer's Association. October, 1973.

Anahid loved playing Solitaire. In Minden, Ontario at a cottage, in the early 2000's.

Anahid posing in her mother Hosanna's belly dance costume in Toronto. Taken by Yousuf Karsh's brother, Cavouk Karsh, in Toronto (via Anahid's friend Arnold Edinborough—who was Editor-In-Chief and later Publisher, at *Saturday Night Magazine*). 1960.

Pierre Berton was a close family friend. Here he is at Preston Lake with Anahid. 1984.

Anahid in London, England. 1950.

Anahid at her typewriter at her home in Aurora, Ontario. Late 1990's.

Anahid (fourth from front left) and Tony (third from left front row) Swann's wedding photograph. Tony's mother, Ruby (second from front left), and his younger brother, Alan Swann (far right front row), also attended. London, England. 1954.

Anahid's Graduation Photo. University of Winnipeg. Bachelor of Arts Honours. 1972.

Anahid exploring Europe. Here she is in Milan. 1949.

Hosanna. Anahid's mother. Middle East (could have been taken in Turkey or Syria). Late 1920's or early 1930's.

Anahid, Toronto area. Late 1950's.

Anahid and Antonia (Smudgie) at Antonia and James' condo at Harbourfront in Toronto taken by a friend. Early 2000's.

Anahid in the Eastern Dance Costume pouring Turkish coffee with two YMCA members as published in the *Globe & Mail* in Toronto. She taught a course there called "The Art of Useless but Enjoyable Living". *Globe & Mail*, January 16, 1960, p.11.

Antonia and Anahid in their backyard on Oakwood Avenue in Winnipeg, Manitoba. May, 1972.

Anahid wrote book reviewes for *The Toronto Telegram* for seven years. She helped develop her role into a TV segment at CFTO-TV (Toronto) with Wellesly Hicks, who was a Telegram feature writer and columnist.

Anahid modelling on the steps of Casa Loma in Toronto. 1959-60.

Anahid wrote on the back of this photo: "*...1952 England August 2nd...'not poppies, not mandragora...' 'my Darling D-D Till we meet, till Death do us join. The End. The Beginning.*" Tony was the love of Anahid's life. England, August 2, 1952.

Hosanna, Anahid's mother. Late 1930's or early 1940's.

Anahid as a young girl with her mother,
Hosanna. Aleppo, Syria. Early or mid-1930's.

A painting of Anahid when she was
a teenager. Aleppo, Syria. 1948.

Anahid & Hosanna. Aleppo, Syria taken at
Diana Studios by Hosanna's photographer.
Early 1930's.

The first President of post-independence Syria, Shukri al-Quwatl, who was in power during the 1940's and 1950's.

Hosanna, Anahid's mother. Late 1920's.

Anahid's best friend from the Francisan Orphange, Number 72, otherwise known as Josephine. Late 1940's.

Anahid & Hosanna in Hosanna's bedroom.
Aleppo, Syria. Mid 1940's.

Anahid modelling in Toronto.
Late 1950's.

Anahid winning the Selfridge's Beauty Contest with the British Actor/ Songwriter Bill Owen at Wembley Stadium. There were 4,000 people in attendance. 1950.

Anahid obtaining her Bachelor's of Education from the University of Manitoba. Winnipeg, Manitoba. 1974.

Anahid worked in the Public Relations Department of British American Oil Company. Toronto, Canada. October 17, 1956.

Anahid (Ann Swann) at her teaching desk at Mazo de la Roche Bilinguial Public School in Newmarket, Ontario. 1989-1990.

James Kreppner, Anahid's son-in-law. Aurora, Ontario. Mid 1990's. James was like a second son to Anahid.

Anahid at her home in Aurora, Ontario, taken by her daugher Antonia (Smudgie). Early 2000's. The sparkles above her head capture the magic energy of Anahid.

Left to right: Peter Swann, Ann Swann, (nee Anahid Hagopian) & Tony Swann. Celebrating Anahid's Bachelor of Education Degree from the University of Manitoba at our home in Fort Rouge, Winnipeg, Manitoba, 1974. This was the start of Anahid's almost 20-year teaching career which spanned until 1992.

ACKNOWLEDGEMENTS

At this point, I would like to express my extreme gratitude to the brilliant Evelyn Elgie and their dedicated team of professionals at Inanna Publications for their dedication to getting my mother's memoir published. I also want to thank the absolute gem of an editor, who is now my friend, Christine Gorden Manley. Even in the moments when I wondered how much longer it would take to find a home for this book, Christine never faltered; she knew the perfect home for it would be found.

I would also like to thank the following amazingly kind people for their thoughtful comments on the book: Karen Bender, Michael Bender, Pierre Berton and his family, David Clipperton, James Kreppner, John Kreppner, Steven Pressfield, Angie Wilkinson and Gwen Yoshiki. I am eternally grateful to all of you.

—Antonia Swann

AUTHOR

Anahid Hagopian began as Orphan Number 86, in Aleppo, Syria. After her single mother, Hosanna, became wealthy by singing and acting on the stage, she rescued Anahid from the orphanage. Anahid went from a world of cruel nuns, poverty, black and white, and silence, to a world of men, comfort, colour, and music. In the years leading up to WWII, Anahid lived under the protective wing of Hosanna, whose main wish was to ensure Anahid's freedom from the male-dominated Middle East. At the end of the war, a British soldier asked Anahid to marry him. Saying goodbye to her mother meant she may never see Hosanna again, but it also meant she would finally have the chance of freedom through education. Decades later, after meeting the love of her life, Tony Swann, Anahid found herself in Canada where, after having Antonia and then Peter and having a series of writing and television jobs, she obtained three graduate degrees. She became the beloved teacher, Ann Swann. Until 1992, Anahid passionately taught French and English to thousands of public-school children, of all ages, both in Manitoba and Ontario, until her retirement, when she refocused on her main love: writing.

EDITOR

Smudgie, whose real name is Antonia Swann, is a singer-songwriter from Toronto, Canada. Her nickname "Smudgie", which her mom gave her, stuck from birth. Born in Gormley, Ontario, Smudgie grew up in Winnipeg, Manitoba, taking guitar lessons with her younger brother Pete from an early age. After her father passed away suddenly when she was fifteen, her family moved back to Ontario. She spent a year as an au pair girl in Paris, France, learning French. She then came back to Toronto, eventually obtaining her Ph.D. in Economics from York University. She lived with her first partner, James Kreppner, from 1982 until his death from tainted blood in 2009. She worked as a Senior Health Economist for the Ontario government and then, when an opportunity arose, she decided to follow her first love and go fulltime into music. Her music has been placed on Major League Baseball, TV shows from around the world, played on terrestrial radio and across America's sports arenas. She has played live in Nashville, including at the Bluebird Café, in London, and in her hometown of Toronto, where she won Best of The Open Mic. She currently lives with her music producer partner David at Harbourfront, where they both create music.